CRUS IN CHAINS

By
Robin Esser

P

Palatino Publishing

First published in 2015 by Palatino Publishing
Copyright © Robin Esser, 2015

Also by Robin Esser:

The Hot Potato (1969)
The Paper Chase (1971)

ISBN: 978-1-907841-14-9

Palatino Publishing 66 Florence Road Brighton BN1
6DJ United Kingdom
palatinobooks@gmail.com

To my family.

DAILY EXPRESS

No. 21,846   MONDAY JULY 21 1969   Weather: Sunny spells; very warm   Price 5d.

2am: 'We'll walk now'

MAN IS ON THE MOON

NEIL ARMSTRONG

EDWIN ALDRIN

DATELINE: Sea of Tranquillity

TWO hours after landing on the moon last night Neil Armstrong and Edwin Aldrin decided that they would step on to the lunar surface at 2 o'clock this morning.

Mission Control in Houston, Texas, signalled: "O.K.—we are ready to support you on that."

(remaining body text not legible)

Within limit

(body text not legible)

Continued on Page 2

And the Russian robot is just 10 miles up

Historic Page One – July 21, 1969

4

INTRODUCTION

I have been in journalism one way or another for some 60 years. I have been a reporter, gossip columnist, feature writer, foreign correspondent, features editor and an editor, including being in charge of one of the nation's biggest Sunday newspapers, an editorial executive and later executive managing editor of the *Daily Mail*. I have clocked up more than fifty years in Fleet Street, which is, I suppose, something of a record. I am a Fellow of the Society of Editors which has Press freedom as its first objective. The way journalists work and the way newspapers are now produced have gone through a seismic change in that time and I have charted those changes while recalling some of the highlights of my career.

When Lord Beaverbrook, who was a Canadian, bought the *Daily Express* and founded the *Sunday Express* he adopted the Crusader as the newspaper's logo. He bought his papers, as he famously remarked, for 'propaganda not profit'. In 1951, as a protest at Parliament's neglect of the old Empire and Imperial free trade and the growing interest in trade and political ties with Europe, he put the Crusader into chains. It was a perceptive move which is echoed today by Britain's troubles with the EU.

All newspapers, from serious broadsheets to red top 'populars' have their own crusades. All newspapers are in chains today as the State becomes more and more powerful and impatient of criticism and endeavours to extend its control over the media. Is this what our democracy now deserves? The democracy that was held up to the world as a model?

No, but it is what we are threatened with. The Press in this country has never enjoyed the freedom bestowed upon the American Press with the First Amendment, which guarantees freedom of the media. Instead in modern times Parliament has steadily chipped away at media freedom with legislation designed to put a chilling effect on investigative journalism and the exposure of those who either misuse public money or abuse their positions of trust in the public eye.

I am thinking of the arrival of CFAs (Conditional Fee Agreements) – the no-win-no-fee arrangements that have escalated the costs of contesting libel actions into millions of pounds; the draconian libel laws themselves, which only now have been the subject of some well overdue reform; Contempt of Court; the Data Protection Act; the Bribery Act; the Harassment Act; the Terrorism Act, among others. And the arrival by the back door of a privacy law based on several judges' views of the Human Rights Act which was introduced to the statute book by Labour.

During the last twenty years the Press has been harried by politicians with inquiry after inquiry into its ethics and practices and it is now regulated and 'self-regulated' to such an extent it is only half-free.

The life blood of local papers reporting local news to inform their communities about what is going on in their name is being blocked. The national papers, struggling to make a profit in the digital age, are emasculated. There are actually strong voices in this country, following the Leveson Inquiry, that are calling for ultimate statutory control of the Press – a promise once made by Labour's Harriet Harman. They deserve a Robert Mugabe in charge of Britain.

Following Leveson's recommendations the laws that protect journalists' sources are to be weakened so that information acquired confidentially can now be seized by police. And Leveson's self-preserving and outrageous recommendation that whistle-blowers should report their misgivings only to the organisation that is running the abuses and never to the media, guarantees that scandals will more rarely be exposed and heralds the possible end of investigative journalism which protects the public by telling them how their money is being spent – or more often misspent.

In the time I have been a Fleet Street journalist the Press has gone through two revolutions. When I started as a reporter there was no such thing as a Press Complaints Commission (PCC). There was no standards code such as there is today— the Editors' Code of Practice. There were no Select Committees prying into matters they did not fully understand; no judicial inquiries. I cannot imagine the Lord Beaverbrook I knew being asked to appear before such a body and then being asked about his children

– as Lord Rothermere was by Leveson. I am still not clear what Lord R's children have to do with the ethics of the Press, particularly as he has often proclaimed his belief in the independence of his editors and never interferes in editorial matters.

Admittedly the atmosphere in Fleet Street in my early days was pretty cavalier. Reporters sent on jobs were expected to get the story. The odd foot would go in the door of someone who was not inclined to co-operate. The public had nobody to whom they could complain – except the editor of the paper the reporters represented. On the other hand there were fewer paparazzi as the markets those itinerant photographers mostly depend upon are the magazines in the United States and in Europe. Some people were upset – not a lot of 'ordinary' people, as the Press does not write about them a great deal – preferring to feature those who are already known to the public.

Bribery? I doubt it was necessary for Percy Hoskins, the great crime reporter of the *Daily Express* in the fifties, to bribe a policeman. He was friendly with most of them. The only story I recall about Percy and the use of alcohol was when he mistakenly fed his canary some cognac and the bird fell off its perch.

The same goes for Chapman Pincher, the greatest post war security-busting journalist of Fleet Street, who knew more about spies than MI5 and MI6 put together and regularly dined with the heads of both organisations. The wine may have been expensive but it did not flow in buckets. What a reporter! I remember, from my brief stay in the War Office getting ready for the Suez Operation as a national serviceman, seeing stickers on the phones reading BE CAREFUL WHAT YOU SAY. CHAPMAN PINCHER MAY BE LISTENING.

Not, I think, an early example of phone hacking. Mobiles had not then been invented and the technology for listening-in was basic, although the local postmistress could ear-wig on any conversation that was put through her manual exchange.

The systems we reporters used and the hot metal process by which the newspapers were printed were primitive compared with today. I used to carry four pennies – the price of a local call – in my pocket to use in a telephone box and I could make a reverse charge call to the office to dictate my copy... usually to a rather cynical but rapid touch typist whose favourite and not very encouraging phrase was 'Is there much more of this?'

Indeed there was one memorable occasion when Robin Stafford, the *Daily Express* man in Athens, who had been thrown out of the country by the military junta which had started a successful coup, managed to sneak back in to Greece. Through a contact at the central telephone exchange and hidden in a cupboard he got a line through to the *Express*. In those days copy-takers who specialised in taking overseas correspondents' copy came to work in the afternoons so, as it was the morning, the foreign desk put him through to a 'home news' copy taker.

He had never heard of Robin Stafford.

'What's your name?'

'Stafford.'

'How do you spell it?'

'For f***s sake get on with it! I'm crouched in a cupboard in Greece.'

'Don't talk to me like that!' roared the copy-taker as he slammed the phone down. It was several days before Stafford could contact the office again.

Today a lap-top, a mobile phone or one of a number of digital hand-held instruments would have given him instant access to the office from anywhere in the world.

I used to have a Post Office bank book in my pocket in case I had to stay overnight in a hotel. Then I could nip out in the morning and draw enough cash to settle the bill. No credit cards then – not even a cheque guarantee card although I always carried a cheque book too.

In the mid-fifties the printed word was all-powerful. Today, the internet, social media such as Twitter and Facebook and TV all dominate. Ironically, as the influence of newspapers has extended far beyond the boundaries of their physical printed circulations through online presence, the independence of those newspapers in this country has been hedged in by new legislation, eroding the freedom of the press to an alarming extent. Our precious democracy itself is in danger on a local, regional, and national level. Few people realise that the Labour Government, almost as its last act in

2010, brought in a law, the Bribery Act, which could – and, given the impact on Members of Parliament, probably would – have prevented the *Telegraph* publishing their MPs' expenses exposé – or at the very least put the editor at serious risk of being dragged into court and thrown into jail. Knowing the calibre of the then editor, Tony Gallagher, I have no doubt he would have taken those risks, but probably at some personal cost.

Then the phone hacking scandal at the *News of the World* hit the headlines – not as a result of a police investigation (which Leveson showed had been woefully inadequate although, with curious logic, he decided it was pursued with 'integrity') but due to the efforts of an investigative journalist on the *Guardian*.

The most sensational allegation was that the *News of the World* had deleted murder victim Millie Dowler's messages on her mobile phone, giving her family the false hope that she was still alive. In fact the police later said this was not true and that the messages had been deleted automatically by her phone provider.

The *Guardian*, which had printed the story, later corrected it – but on page 32 even though it had been on their front page. Thus the correction was hardly noticed by anyone, but the damage had been done and in the wake of the furore the Prime Minister saw his chance.

Because David Cameron had rashly and, against much advice, appointed Andy Coulson, former *News of the World* editor, as his head of communications at Number Ten, he took the cynical course of appointing a judicial inquiry into the whole of Press ethics in order to take attention away from his own mistake.

At huge expense to the tax-payer and to the media industry itself the Leveson Inquiry probed the wildest of allegations and listened to a self-obsessed troupe of over-theatrical celebrities moaning about the 'intrusion' they had suffered while building up their not inconsiderable fortunes with the help of the publicity they had received from the very newspapers about which they were now complaining. The Inquiry was assisted by a panel of assessors, not one of whom had ever served on a popular best-selling newspaper. It also managed to bite back at its instigator – exposing the Prime Minister's cosy relationship with News International, Rupert Murdoch and his chief executive at News International, Rebekah Brooks.

Had there ever previously been such excruciating communication between a newspaper executive (Rebekah) and a leading politician (Cameron) as her e-mail 'We are in this together. Yes you Cam'? Has a prime minister of Great Britain ever had three close friends involved in a criminal trial? Has any prime minister ridden a police horse given to a media executive?

The whole Inquiry was set up on a deliberate lie- 'that the public has lost faith in the PCC'. No evidence whatsoever has backed this suggestion which was swallowed wholesale by Leveson. There was no indication that the readers had lost faith in the way in which newspapers were 'regulated'. No sign they had stopped reading and enjoying the Press; no sign they had ceased to buy newspapers.

More likely a majority had never heard of the PCC and those who had, and used it, were, according to professional independent surveys, largely happy with the service they received.

We now know that, although Leveson was aware of the much wider use of phone hacking by lawyers, insurance companies and the police themselves, he chose to limit his inquiry to his brief of investigating the ethics of the Press. How very judge-like!

Against the enormous changes for newspapers I have outlined my professional life, which has been enlivened by a succession of lucky chances, and the story has a setting that readers may find has an historical significance.

Of course, the end of that story is yet to come. Will news still be printed on pulped trees in another fifty years? Will the police continue to arrest journalists for doing their job? Will the State finally succeed in silencing its rumbustious critics? Will politicians be allowed to fiddle their expenses at the public's cost?

I need a crystal ball to answer those questions. But if newspapers go entirely online and global what will be the point of regulation which applies only to this country?

Already *Mail Online*, now the world's most-read newspaper on the web, is being pushed to obey British regulation even though it has an American home page and the majority of its readers are Americans.

1
BEGINNINGS

It all began when I was about nine or ten and stopped wanting to drive a train or a fire engine when I grew up. I discovered our neighbours in Dewsbury, West Yorkshire, were the parents of Harold Keeble – then a Fleet Street giant on Lord Beaverbrook's mighty *Daily Express*. Although I had not met him and was not to do so for some years Harold's proud mother's stories about her son convinced me that I wanted to be a newspaper man too.

I started a newsletter called the *Northfields Gazette*, after the street in which we lived and persuaded my mother to be its 'printer' and manager and reproduce the copies she and I delivered to doubtless unappreciative neighbours, giving the latest on the local council's plans to tarmac our un-adopted private road and remove the barrier at its end, along with snippets on the growing of produce in the allotments on the other side of our street.

With the true arrogance and ignorance of childhood I promised my mother, who was a remarkably clever woman, that I would one day edit her favourite newspaper – then the great *Sunday Express*.

Nearly forty years or so later I did. Alas she was no longer alive but I think she would have looked down with pleasure that my promise had come to pass and I always think how lucky I was to have been born to such a woman.

Our neighbours heard that I wanted to be a journalist and Mrs Keeble told me: 'Harold will help you.'

That was the second piece of luck. Harold certainly did – in more ways than one. The first time was when, at the age of sixteen, I went down to London to ask him for his advice on pursuing my chosen career. Ordered by his mother to see me he met me in the hall of the prestigious art-deco building in Fleet Street with its silver snakes winding up the steps to the lifts, its murals, its Epstein bust of Beaverbrook, and its forbidding black glass. The 'Black Lubyanka' was how it was known

I knew Harold had joined the local paper, the *Dewsbury Reporter*, straight from school as an apprentice and I wanted to know if that was the best route for me or if I should try to get to university. The masters at the Wheelwright Grammar School in Dewsbury – to which Harold had gone and where I was then – had suggested I might make Leeds university or, if I worked very hard, maybe Manchester.

'If you can get to Oxford or Cambridge,' Harold told me on my visit to London, 'you will make contacts there that will last you your life. If you can't, don't bother with the other places. Just get a job with the local paper and learn your trade as I did.'

It was some of the best advice I ever had. I returned to Dewsbury and the Wheelwright

16

Grammar School determined to go to Oxford. The headmaster was dismissive of my ambition and the school declined to help. They thought I had no chance and it had been several years since any pupil from my school had got to Oxbridge.

I researched the matter myself and found that the Oxford colleges ran entrance exams, one set for each cluster of two or three colleges. These exams did not need your school to enter you for them. I discovered I could apply myself. I put in for three separate clusters and spent some very nervous but exciting days staying down in Oxford and doing my best.

Eventually two colleges – Hertford and Wadham -- offered me a place. I chose Wadham because its then Warden was the prominent classics scholar and wit Sir Maurice Bowra. I think in retrospect that the college was eager to leaven the usual public schoolboy entrants with a few lads from grammar schools to show how democratic they were. If that was so I, a green and callow youth from the West Riding of Yorkshire, was the beneficiary.

I had not been at Oxford for many weeks when I fell in with some fellow students who had decided that Oxford needed a university newspaper. Astonishingly, although Cambridge had *Varsity*, Oxford had no newspaper, only student magazines. So this group, Clive Labovitch, Michael Heseltine and Earl White, bought a small literary magazine called *Cherwell* and re-launched it as a newspaper. I was its first news editor and its first editor was an undergraduate from Brasenose College called Mike

Pike, who later had a distinguished career in the Foreign Office, was knighted and became Her Majesty's Ambassador to Vietnam.

Clive and Earl were given some very sound advice on the distribution of *Cherwell* by a young Australian undergraduate called Rupert Murdoch but he had to return home as his father had died that year. Rupert was succeeded as our circulation man by John Heyman who went on to become Elizabeth Taylor's agent and whose favourite warm-up party trick was to open the metal crown stoppers of beer bottles between his teeth.

My first challenge when I was made editor was to repulse the invasion of Cambridge's newspaper *Varsity* with its 'Oxford edition'. *Varsity* was edited then by Michael Winner, who became the successful film maker and controversial food critic. We simply printed a Cambridge edition and rushed it over to the Other Place.

Like the two freebies in London fifty years later we came to the joint conclusion that the competition was too expensive to last.

Luck again played its part in my first story to hit the nationals. Several fire engines came steaming past College, sirens blaring, and I jumped on my bike and followed them. The Clarendon Laboratory was on fire. As this was where the early research on splitting the atom was carried out and there were fears of radio activity I found the nearest telephone box, inserted my four copper pennies and dictated the story to most of the major newspapers.

My report was carried in five Fleet Street papers. I was paid the then significant sum of £25, £12 of which I spent on buying a 1927 Austin Seven with a removable top which Sarah Rothschild, one of *Cherwell*'s female undergraduate columnists, named 'Tweetie Pie'. It was not a very modern machine and its radiator leaked, needing to be topped up with a raw egg for any long journeys. Still, the breakfast like smell was some consolation.

I did other things than run *Cherwell*. I really did some academic work, studying history with my charismatic tutor Pat Thompson, whose brother was a distinguished journalist, and I studied, as my special subject, Indian history in the age of Warren Hastings, with Dame Lucy Sutherland principal of the then all girls college Lady Margaret Hall. I got a degree with honours at the end. I also rowed a bit and played hockey for Wadham. This led me to another bit of luck.

In those Oxford days the rules about locking up colleges were strict. If you came back late you had to climb back into college and hope no one caught you. One night after a long sojourn playing hockey and celebrating in Cambridge I reached Wadham at about one in the morning. Climbing in over the wall of the Warden's garden I was lifted from the cabbage patch by Sir Maurice Bowra himself as he took a stroll in the night air.

'Report to my lodgings at noon,' he boomed.

Next day I duly did just that. But as I knocked at the door an agitated man in a tweed suit arrived and added to my knock. It was Evelyn Waugh. The great novelist was furious that he had just been refused permission by the college porter to view a Holman Hunt painting which had been newly installed in his old college, Keble, on the jobsworth grounds that he, Waugh, was not an MA of the university.

Waugh blurted out this news as the Warden opened the door. Sir Maurice looked at us both and said: 'Mr Esser, take Mr Waugh into my study and pour him a large drink while I finish the telephone call I am engaged in at the moment.'

I did so and I never got the telling-off the Warden intended to give me. I did get a three and a half hour lunch accompanied by fine wines in the company of one of greatest wits in the university and one of our most important authors. I also got a slight hangover and a memory to last a lifetime. And I got a great diary story that led the William Hickey gossip column in the *Express* next day

All this journalistic activity attracted the attention of Fleet Street – much to the joy of half a dozen of us who thought adding to our student grants with the odd cheque from a newspaper was a very good idea.

We put our heads together and decided to form the Oxford University Press Club with the idea of asking prominent journalists to come and talk to us. I was put in charge of the invitations and this was where Harold Keeble came to help me once again. The first person I asked to talk to us was, of course, Harold. He accepted – then at the last minute sent Anne Scott James, then a columnist on the *Sunday*

Express and later the mother of Sir Max Hastings. Anne was fascinating and gracious. A wonderful substitute.

For the second meeting I again invited Harold. Again he accepted. Again he withdrew at the last minute but sent another great journalist in his place. Harold never did address our Press Club but he continued to send us distinguished figures from Fleet Street.

One of those was the news editor of the *Sunday Express*, Bernard Drew. Bernard, who became a good friend, invited me and Mike Pike to work as casual reporters for the *Sunday Express* on Saturdays when their usual staff compliment was swollen by extra people.

Ah! That luck again. We were sent by Bernard to Wimbledon to try to interview Jaroslav Drobny, the tennis star who had defected to the West from communist Czechoslovakia to try talking to him on the eve of the 1954 final in which he was to play the Australian ace Ken Rosewall. The idea was that, if we could get him to the phone, the *Sunday Express* office would contact his mother back in Prague, patch the call through, and he could speak to her and hear her good wishes.

Amazingly we succeeded. Drobny was close to tears as he had not seen his mother for some years. But I am convinced the boost that conversation gave him had a tremendous effect and he beat the favourite Rosewall in four sets to win the greatest Grand Slam of his life. Drobny thanked both of us afterwards and gave me a signed tennis ball to mark his appreciation of what we had done.

Bernard was so pleased by the success of his protégé that he offered me a regular Saturday 'double shift' – 10am to 10pm – for which I was paid eight guineas (£8.40p in today's money). Every Saturday during term I would take the early excursion train from Oxford to Paddington for a great experience.

An additional excitement occurred when the rival newspapers came in during the evenings and we had to chase up stories they had that the *Sunday Express* had missed. On one occasion one of the red tops had a story and picture of a boy who, armed with his bow and arrow, had scared off a man intent on robbing his mother's shop. We had covered the story but the reporter concerned was eager to get to another tip-off he thought was more interesting and had been impatient with the mother, not allowing her to tell of her son's heroic act. By the second edition we too had the story and the picture and the impatient reporter had a warning letter from the news editor.

One assignment I was sent on proved to be less successful. I was despatched to watch former Prime Minister Clem Attlee's house in Buckinghamshire as there was a rumour he was unwell and was going to be transferred to hospital that day. My instruction was to phone the news desk before afternoon conference at 3pm. The nearest public phone box that would take my four pennies was half a mile away. I reached it, told the office there was nothing doing and trudged back to the house – only to find that while I was away the ambulance had arrived and whisked the great statesman away. Mobile phones were then not even dreamed of. But all this journalistic experience was to lead me on a remarkable adventure as a 'guest' of Her Majesty the Queen.

2
CALL-UP

The 'gap year' had not been invented then. We had two years National Service. I had deferred mine until after university and I joined KOYLI, the Kings Own Yorkshire Light Infantry, at Strensall Green near York for basic training. The Regimental Sergeant Major was a fearsome fellow whose favourite phrase concerned our green berets and our hat badge – a silver bugle (the smallest in the British army). 'That badge,' the RSM roared, 'wants to shine like a jewel in a pheasant's arsehole.' It did!

In the bathrooms of the depot there were no plugs as the recruits had stolen them for subsequent use. I suggested to the Medical Officer – also doing his National Service but bearing a senior rank as a captain – that every recruit should be issued with a plug on arrival. This resulted in a huge energy saving as the hot water no longer just washed away down the plug hole!

After basic drill was over I went on to Officer Training School at Eaton Hall near Chester, an institution with an even more alarming RSM. The building that housed the officer cadets was the old stately home of the Dukes of Westminster. It had been taken over by the War Office in 1947 to accommodate the National Service intake of potential officers and the Westminsters had abandoned it to the army.

Hanging above the staircase was an old dirty painting of voluptuous nudes with a few stains that exuberant cadets had caused by throwing tomatoes at the figures on display, plus one or two bayonet holes. Imagine my surprise and delight in telling the story a few years later in 1959 in the *Daily Express* for which I was then working, when the very same painting (skilfully restored) came up for auction and achieved a then record price of £275,000.

Major Alfred Ernest Allnatt, a British millionaire, bought the 1634 masterpiece, *The Adoration of the Magi* by Rubens, from the Westminster estate and presented it to King's College Cambridge to hang in the chapel – where it is today. As the stains and years of neglect had been cleaned it is more appreciated by the students of the college than it was by us! But when I am in Cambridge I pop into King's to admire it.

At Eaton Hall I met a young Royal Marine called Mike Turk. His family have been watermen on the Thames since the reign of the first Queen Elizabeth and have provided the Sovereigns with Swan Masters for ever. Mike, once out of the Marines, realised that his father's business of hiring rowing boats and putt-putt motor boats in the Thames at Kingston needed updating. He was asked to provide the boats for the first TV film of *Swallows and Amazons*, the classic children's book by Arthur Ransom. It was the start of a new career that has included supplying flying boats for James Bond films and the replica frigate that he built for the

Hornblower TV series and took the role of Nelson's *Victory* in the battle of Trafalgar re-enactment in the Solent in 2005. Mike remains a close and loyal friend to this day.

One particular activity at Eaton Hall was exhausting. We were chosen to represent the Hall in an assault course competition to be held against teams from the other officer training establishments, Sandhurst and Mons. Determined to win we were put through the course before breakfast, after breakfast and before supper every day. We did win! When we all 'passed out' of OCTU and were commissioned we went our several ways and I left for Cyprus on anti-Eoka duty.

Then luck played its part again. I had no sooner settled into a dugout in the Troodos Mountains with a comforting bottle of Scotch that I shared with my squaddies, than I got a call to report back to the War Office in London. The Suez crisis was cooking up following the Egyptian President Nasser's unilateral 'nationalisation' of the Franco-British built and owned Suez Canal, the important short cut for trade shipping between the Mediterranean and the Far East. An Army battle group was being formed for possible intervention in Egypt and the Army needed public relations officers who were fit enough to go on active service and accompany the world's Press corps who would go into Egypt with the invading force. Army policy up to then had been to employ disabled officers in PR so the War Office had scrolled through the lists of national service officers with journalistic experience and who were fit enough to do the job.

They came up with two. Me and a lad I had first met very briefly on the cricket pitch of my school in Dewsbury when his school in Barnsley had played ours. He was a very competent batsman, with hopes of playing for the Yorkshire first XI and he had worked on a local Yorkshire newspaper. Michael Parkinson was his name. He was a second lieutenant in the Pay Corps stationed at Catterick. Parky and I were brought together at the War Office to form a unit to accompany the battle group and we were given a commanding officer with one arm and a number two with one eye. No prizes for guessing who was going to war while the senior officers played 'a strategic role'.

However the politicians were wavering and most of our unit – the vehicles and radio vans and their drivers and the cooks – sailed under my tender command for Malta to wait for the orders to invade while Parky flew to Cyprus to organise arrangements for the Press corps.

Luck was with me again as a big story broke on the island in October 1956. Many of the men in the 3rd Battalion of the Grenadier Guards, also camped in Malta, were Z Reservists, plucked from their civilian jobs and recalled for the invasion force. Unfortunately Army pay lagged far behind civilian pay and the reservists' families were left back in the UK struggling to make ends meet and feed the children on a few pounds a week. The reservists themselves were fed up hanging around in temporary accommodation waiting for the politicians to decide whether they were going to fight. The pressure on the men was huge and there were open demonstrations and even spoken threats of mutiny. Guards Mutiny… What a headline for Fleet Street!

A plane load of reporters and photographers landed in Malta to be met by the only Army PR officer on the island at the time – me. I picked up the journalists at the airport in a coach, suitably equipped with cold beers, towels and swimming costumes and bussed them, via a pleasant beach, to the headquarters of the regiment on the island. I had arranged with the CO for the soldiers to explain all their grievances, openly and fully, with no officers or NCOs present. This was very successful and I took the reporters and photographers back to the airport fully briefed. The resulting stories were sympathetic and actually stirred the authorities back home to help the families in distress.

A day or so later General Sir Hugh Stockwell, in charge of the invasion force, flew into Malta. He called for the PR officer responsible for what he judged a job well done. When I presented myself in the uniform of the General Services Corps which I now had to wear and with one pip on my shoulder the General looked me up and down and asked: 'What are you?'

'Your public relations officer Sir,' I replied. 'I am doing my National Service.'

'Tweetie Pie' – the Austin 7 that I bought with part of my earnings from reporting the Clarendon Laboratory fire.

On active service in Port Said. Promoted to captain, but swapping the peaked cap for a beret in order to present less of an obvious target!

Stockwell was a very charismatic soldier with a great sense of fairness. He turned to his ADC and asked: 'What rank do these chaps normally have if they are doing this job?'

'Captain, sir,' came the reply.

'Well make him a bloody captain then,' said Stockwell.

'Excuse me, sir,' I said, rather naughtily. 'But there are two of us. Second Lieutenant Parkinson is in Cyprus organising the advance band of correspondents.'

'Same for him,' said Stockwell to his ADC. 'I want my men properly rewarded.'

That was how we became the two youngest serving captains in the British Army at that time. Michael never knew the whole story until he came to write his best-selling autobiography *Parky* and we lunched together years later to go over the early days.

Meanwhile the summer rains came down like monsoons in Malta and I ordered all my unit to dig trenches round their tents to prevent the water washing in and ruining all their possessions. For this I was hauled before the General Officer Commanding in Malta, a major-general, who complained I had ruined their rugger pitches on which we were camped! Rather cheekily I asked if he preferred to let my chaps get wet.

When I told the commanding officer of an Armoured Brigade whose Centurion tanks were parked on the island's polo ground, about this he said; 'We will show them! Come tonight and we will play musical chairs with six tanks and five places to pitch for.'

It was the noisiest game of musical chairs I have ever played; it woke up most of the island as the tanks crashed into each other with music playing over their radios, and left the polo ground an expanse of muddy heaps and gouges. But it was fun for us. And I think the GOC got the message.

At last came the orders to invade. I dropped in to Port Said with the advance troops on day one with two reporters, with Fleet Street's finest a few hours behind me and Parky and I left on the last day which was a few days before Christmas 1956.

Our weeks in Port Said were a mixture of frustration, danger and excitement. We set up a Press Centre in a block of flats and bussed the reporters to General Stockwell's headquarters for regular Press briefings. One of the reporters was Sandy Gall, then working for Reuters and later a star of ITV's News at Ten. Sandy also became celebrated for his adventures with the Mujahedeen in Afghanistan and he became a life-long friend.

The army allowance for our Press corps was a bottle of spirits per man per month. For the thirsty reporters from Fleet Street this was woefully inadequate so we set up regular flights to Cyprus to bring over much needed supplies. Then we found the old French Club hidden behind boards set up to protect its windows and, cowering inside, the club's chief waiter. We soon persuaded him to open up for the Press (and ourselves) and we all did serious damage to his surviving stock of Champagne.

While the early days of the conflict were marked by scattered resistance and carried the threat of Egyptian snipers the ceasefire forced upon then Prime Minister Anthony Eden by the Americans and President Eisenhower, who did not approve of the action, changed the atmosphere into one of sullen acceptance by the local population and increasing boredom for the Press. This was broken suddenly and tragically. One of the cadets with whom I had been commissioned at Eaton Hall was Anthony Moorhouse. As we had gone through the same tortures and training together, we had become friends. Moorhouse was the son of the head of the eponymous jam-making firm in Leeds, a distant relative of the Queen, and now a National Service second lieutenant in the West Yorkshire regiment on duty in Port Said. On patrol in the city in his Land Rover, armed but alone, he was surrounded by militant Egyptians and kidnapped.

I joined in the house-to-house hunt for him but no one could find him. The United Nations, which had brokered the cease fire, contacted President Nasser who tried to find out what had happened to Moorhouse. Eventually his body was found – he had been hidden in a metal box, with a gag round his mouth and he had suffocated. The incident, fully reported by the world's news outlets, aroused furious anger in Britain, leading to extensive criticism of the government, especially by Hugh

Gaitskell who was not only the Leader of the Opposition but also an MP for Leeds, home of the Moorhouse family. For Eden it was another blow to his authority following Eisenhower's disapproval of the decision to invade Egypt. For the British Empire and our imperial reputation the whole botched Suez campaign was a significant nail in the coffin.

But for me it was another step up the ladder of my Fleet Street ambitions. By the time Parky and I left Port Said at the end of December 1956 there was hardly a top reporter or a columnist in Fleet Street I did not know. Once back in London the Army decided I should go to Germany to join the PR team at the HQ of the British Army of the Rhine in Munchen Gladbach.

A few weeks later another slice of that luck. The Army PR officer stationed at the British Embassy – then in Bonn – fell ill. His responsibilities were to liaise between the British Army and the German civil authorities. It seemed I was the only qualified PR officer who spoke some German so I was sent down to take his place. As I was replacing a major and it was necessary to impress the Germans, I was made an acting major. Some progress for an army career that had lasted scarcely 20 months.

One of the Reuters men now stationed there was my friend Sandy Gall. We resumed our friendship and we even shared a bachelor flat for a time on the banks of the great river Rhine.

Sandy's nose had been broken in a rugby game for his university – Aberdeen -- and this caused him to snore loudly. Our peace was regularly disturbed if Sandy had brought a girl-friend back and she decided she could stand the noise no longer and rose in anger to go somewhere where she could spend a peaceful time in a bed of her own.

Bonn was conveniently close to Cologne, a city with a considerable reputation and a lively cultural element. I could often visit the Opera House there as the military attaché had a box and would lend it to me. However one visit to the cemetery was a less happy occasion. I and an Army cameraman had been sent there to photograph the grave of a British soldier for the Imperial War Graves commission. We inadvertently entered through the civilian section and I found myself surrounded by many hundreds of graves of people called Esser – a common name in that part of Germany. I felt quite uneasy.

Another task was agreeing with the German police the route that one of our armoured divisions would take when it left its base in the northern part of the country to undertake manoeuvres many miles away. I consulted the commanding officer of the tank regiment and we came up with a route we thought was safe for the transport of twenty heavy Centurion tanks, carried on a convoy of low-loaders.

The Germans would not accept our route and altered it so part of the journey would be on the autobahn. I asked them if they were sure the bridges on the route would take the weight and they said all would be OK. Off went the tanks on a warm summer's day. They came to a long bridge on the motorway. The first four low loaders went over but the fifth did not. The bridge cracked, then wavered and then crumbled. Fortunately the driver and his companion were not seriously injured. The queue of cars rapidly built up – several miles both ways. Motorways hardly existed in those days except in the States and Germany. A queue of cars such as this was unknown.

The aerial pictures went round the world and appeared in every British newspaper. I had wisely kept my exchanges with the German authorities to show my original route and my doubts about its revision. I later enjoyed a few beers with the local police chiefs who were generous about the affair.

In retrospect I did enjoy my military service but then I was fortunate to be stationed in interesting areas and my experiences in the Suez crisis and later in Nato and the British Army of the Rhine gave me the material to write two novels a few years later.

The first, *The Hot Potato*, was a fictional account of the actual collusion between the west and Israel over the Suez Canal invasion. The second, The *Paper Chase*, was based around a Nato crisis when a missile went missing… Fiction because I had signed the Official Secrets Act. My publisher, Michael Joseph, was very helpful and supportive and the books, which were well reviewed, gave me enough spare cash for a deposit on a sea-going boat that gave me and my young family many hours of enjoyment and an ever-lasting love of Holland where we would spend time afloat most summers.

3

A HACK IN FLEET STREET

It was not difficult for me, once I had completed my two years in the Army, to begin a Fleet Street career in earnest. I returned to the *Sunday Express* as a regular Saturday news desk man and I freelanced as a reporter on several newspapers. One of those was the *Daily Sketch* where I joined Fred Newman, an old University chum, on the gossip diary and first met David English who was to become one of the best-known editors in Fleet Street and a great personal friend. An invitation came into the *Sketch* one day to attend the opening of a new 'theatre revue bar' in the West End and I was sent along with a young photographer just down from Scotland called Harry Benson. When we reached the venue and found it was Soho's soon-to-be-famous strip club – Raymond's Revue Bar – Harry's Scottish puritanism came to the fore.

'I'm not going in there with all those naked women,' he said. 'You go in and I'll sit out here and read a book!'

But my luck was about to appear again…

In the auditorium I saw two rows of Chelsea Pensioners in full uniform, medals gleaming on their chests. I told Paul Raymond, the man in charge, that I would pay for the drinks if his girls would take a pint of beer for each pensioner during the interval, and sit on their laps while they drank it.

As the lasses were wearing only tiny briefs and had tassels hanging from their nipples that would be likely to get entangled with the old soldiers' medals, I knew it would make a great photograph for the *Sketch*. No problem. I rushed outside and told Harry he had to come in and take this picture. It made the centre spread, but when I told the Governor of the Royal Hospital what had happened he groaned.

'I thought it was just an innocent invitation to a respectable establishment,' he said. 'What can I say?'

I suggested that he said: 'I hope the chaps enjoyed themselves. They are all heroes...' And he took my advice.

Harry went on to fame and fortune in New York as one the most distinguished photographers in his field, taking pictures for *Life* and *People* magazines in America. President Ronald Reagan posed for him and he was the man who photographed the Beatles' first sensational tour of America when he captured the iconic picture of the group engaging in a rollicking pillow fight in their bedroom. He also photographed the assassination of Bobby Kennedy.

His ability to get on with the great and the good was well-known and I had a demonstration of that when I was on assignment in the US with him many years later. Bobby's widow, Ethel Kennedy, was to make her first public appearance after that tragedy by attending a charity event at the gated house of a millionaire in Long Island. The whole area round the front door was occupied by reporters, cameramen, and TV crews.

'Come with me,' said Harry. 'When she sees me Ethel will stop outside the gates and have a word. We will get exclusive pictures and you will get exclusive quotes.'

It happened just as Harry predicted. The big black limo with darkened windows stopped at Harry's wave. A window wound down and Ethel Kennedy poked her head out. 'Good to see you Harry,' she said. 'Click away.'

I asked her how she was feeling and why she was supporting the charity the visit was all about. We chatted for a few minutes and the car moved off down the drive. The waiting Press at the door got short shrift and we had our exclusive picture and caption.

In 2009 Harry was appointed CBE for his work behind the camera – a long way from the Glasgow in which he was born – though he has never lost his native accent. Harry and his lovely wife Gigi remain close friends to this day.

I was still working on the *Sunday Express* news desk at the weekends and as soon as my combined salary reached £20 a week I proposed to the girl I had met years before in Dewsbury. Shirley and I married at the start of 1959. Then another chance came my way, I was offered a staff job as reporter on the William Hickey column – then the most powerful and sought after gossip column in the country, occupying the top of page three of the broadsheet *Daily Express* every day of the week. Me – an ordinary young man from a grammar school in

Yorkshire... But my experience at university and in the army had given me a degree of confidence that helped me sail through the rounds of meeting dukes and millionaires, countesses and actresses, singers and celebs. Somehow (I cannot recall just how), I had acquired the bedside telephone number of the notorious Duchess of Argyll...

This was at a time when self-regulation in the form of the Press Council, which later became the Press Complaints Commission, had not been invented. Nor had Rupert Murdoch's *Sun* newspaper. The *Daily Express* was selling 4,250,000 copies a day and bestrode the middle market. Only the *Daily Mirror* out-sold it. Of course the libel laws were strict and dangerous in those days and the rich – the only people who could afford to sue – used them frequently. And I was writing about them every day! You needed to be sure of your facts.

The burden of proof is reversed in libel laws – that means you are not innocent until proved guilty. In fact Sue, Grabbit and Runne say that you, the defending journalist and newspaper, are guilty unless you can prove you are innocent.

However even then the evils of hundred-per-cent uplift success fees for the lawyers representing those allegedly defamed had not been introduced. Those were the invention of the Labour government of 1997 to 2010 in a well-meaning though totally misguided attempt to allow those with limited means to have access to libel justice. All they achieved was a rich gravy train for claimant lawyers able to charge the media up to £800 an hour for the services of a solicitor and more for the services of a QC and provide those rich and powerful people with free and frequent access to a system they could well afford to pay for themselves.

The obvious fact is that very few people who are not wealthy are libelled by national newspapers as they are not generally the subject of much media attention. Thus utterly disproportionate costs are incurred by lawyers representing those allegedly maligned. For example, one MP sued the *Mail* newspapers over an allegation that he had behaved in an arrogant manner to a security guard in Parliament when challenged to produce his ID – which he had forgotten. The MP was awarded the modest sum of £5,000 damages. It cost the paper nearly £1,000,000 to fight the case.

At the start of the present decade America thought our libel laws so out of date, so unjust, so open to abuse that they passed laws shielding US citizens against decisions in the British libel courts and even the United Nations Human Rights Commission reported that it considered our libel laws to be in contravention of Human Rights. Thus were our legislators regarded in contempt by the rest of the civilised world.

Only at the start of 2014 were these laws amended to give better protection to freedom of speech and those who express an opinion. This after a debate that lasted more than thirteen years, which I know so well, as I was invited by the then Minister of Justice,

Jack Straw, to join a panel made up of claimant lawyers, media lawyers, academics and journalists to consider and recommend reforms. The debate was long and heated and lasted for weeks; its chairman, Rowena Collins-Rice, did miracles in producing a report with which we could all agree.

4

THE HICK IN HICKEY

I was put in charge of the William Hickey column in 1963 and there followed, as usual, a series of breaks that did my career no harm. One day in the Black Lubyanka I answered the phone and an aristocratic voice said: 'Marlborough here. That awful chap Bedford has been round Blenheim writing "Woburn is better" on our brochures and giving them to our visitors. That's the sort of thing you like to print in your newspaper isn't it?' And he put the phone down without further conversation.

I immediately feared this was a hoax call from one of my more mischievous friends as the Duke of Marlborough was not given to talking to journalists. I called Blenheim Palace and got the butler. He, rather haughtily, said: 'His Grace never talks to the Press.'

I said I thought he might have done so this time and asked him to check with the Duke. But, 'His Grace is in the bath and cannot be disturbed.'

'Look,' I said, 'the Duke asked me to publish something and he will be very cross with you and with me if you do not ask him to confirm it... Very cross indeed.'

'I will ring you back.'

A somewhat chastened butler later confirmed that it was indeed His Grace, the Duke of Marlborough who had phoned me.

I immediately rang the more approachable and publicity seeking Duke of Bedford and put the charge to him.

'Quite right, old boy, I did,' said Bedford. 'And Woburn *is* better!'

I sent a motorcyclist to Blenheim in Oxfordshire to pick up a brochure and then ride over to Woburn in Bedfordshire, to get it signed and brought back to Fleet Street. It made a great Hickey lead with a page one cross-reference.

Lord Beaverbrook, who took a great personal interest in the column, rang to say how much he had enjoyed the tale. He was not always quite so straightforward with his comments. Several times he would telephone and say: 'Very good story in your column this morning Mr Esser. I hope it is true.'

'I believe so Lord Beaverbrook,' was always my reply.

'Good. I am lunching with him today,' he would sometimes bark, and put the phone down.

That could ruin my lunch. But once it ran in my favour.

I had become quite close to the amazingly wealthy oil magnate Paul Getty and his personal assistant Robina Lund, clever daughter of Sir Thomas Lund, the man who devised the Legal Aid system. I had written a story about the authenticity of a painting Paul Getty had bought many years before from a stack of works on an art gallery floor. I had found some evidence that it was a masterpiece though doubt had always been heaped upon it.

Getty was so taken with that article he invited my wife and me to take tea at Sutton Place, his magnificent country mansion near Guildford, to view the painting concerned. My wife was rather nervous when she found out she had to pour from a Meissen porcelain teapot that must have been worth as much as our modest house in East Molesey. She managed it with only the smallest of trembles.

A little later Robina called me to say that Paul wanted to have lunch with me as he had a problem he thought I could help with. Paul and I met at Trader Vic's in the Hilton Hotel on Park Lane. He explained to me that a lady called Marie, the widow of a dear friend whose children he had helped educate, had moved into Sutton Place and was devoting herself to helping him with the internal décor of the house but was also dropping hints about getting married to him.

'I like her very much,' said Paul. 'But I have done with marriage. Tried it several times but to be honest I am married to the oil business. However I just don't know how to tell her this. I'm too embarrassed to ask her to leave the house.'

I suggested that I ran an interview with him in the Hickey column in which I would make it plain he was never going to marry again – headline: 'I'm married to an oil rag!' says fabulously rich Paul Getty'.

That should give her pause for thought, I said. The piece ran. A day later Paul Getty rang me and said: 'You have done marvels...'

He continued: 'Marie and I were guests of Lord Beaverbrook at Cherkley last night. At the dinner table Marie launched an attack on you, complaining to Max that he employed this journalist called Esser who had printed lies about me in his newspaper.'

Beaverbrook had listened and then turned to the tycoon:

'What do you say about the article, Paul?'

'Max,' said Getty, 'there have been many articles printed about me in my seven decades of life. This was the only one that was a hundred per cent correct.'

At that, Paul told me, 'Marie stood up, threw her napkin down and stormed out. When I got back to Sutton Place later that night she had packed her cases and left! Thank you so much. You are welcome with your family to come to Sutton Place and enjoy the swimming pool and the grounds at any time.'

Paul had a reputation for meanness – hence the tale of him installing a pay phone at Sutton Place so his visitors would pay for their own telephone calls. But, though he clearly did not enjoy others spending his money I never found him mean or grumpy and we stayed in touch for the rest of his life.

I was down in Monte Carlo one summer writing a column from this popular watering hole on the Med. I was staying in a room of the Hotel de Paris which overlooked the harbour when I saw the spectacular yacht, *Christina* which belonged to multi-millionaire Aristotle Onassis, coming in to moor. I lifted the phone and asked the hotel operator to patch me in to the ship's on-board phone. A deep and instantly recognisable voice answered.

'Mr Onassis,' I said 'I write the William Hickey column for Lord Beaverbrook's *Daily Express* and I would like to have a few words with you.'

'I thought William Hickey wrote that column,' he replied.

Now I had recently bought *William Hickey's Collected Diaries* so I was able to correct his mistaken belief.

I told him how Beaverbrook and the column's first writer, Tom Driberg, had named the column in honour of a rumbustious lawyer called Hickey who worked for the East India Company, made a fortune, and regularly caught the clap in the brothels of Covent Garden or the sampans of Hong Kong. He had written a series of revealing memoirs in the early 1800s that were a great read.

There was a pause. 'I'd like to hear more about that William Hickey,' said Onassis. 'So be my guest. I will send the barge over to pick you up at the quayside.'

Thus I met this fabulously wealthy Greek shipping tycoon – and also his on-board companion, Maria Callas, the international opera star who was sipping fruit juice in the yacht's stateroom. Both were fascinated by the salty tales of the original William Hickey and it all made good copy for the column. Later, of course, Onassis married Jack Kennedy's widow, Jacqueline Bouvier Kennedy – in the process, I understand, breaking Maria Callas' heart

One of my most prolific contacts in the diary was a young impecunious debs' delight called Nigel Dempster. He would phone me – often from the butler's pantry of a stately home where he was dining – with entertaining snippets about the other guests or the host and hostess for which we paid him in cash that he would later pop into the office to collect.

One day he told me he wanted to be a gossip writer and asked whether he could come and work on Hickey. I started him on a casual day shift basis – paid by the days he worked. He often complained, then, and later after he had become well-known, that I paid him so little he had to work six days a week to make ends meet.

Around this time I was also introduced by a mutual friend to a young Guards officer called Patrick Lichfield – actually the Earl of Lichfield. He told me the story of how he had watched his troops, on guard at Buckingham Palace, scoop up gravel from the forecourt and sell it in jam jars to tourists gathered outside. This led him to get a spare bearskin, stamp his coat of arms inside, and sell it to an American visitor for enough money to buy a Leica camera.

It was now, he told me, his ambition to leave the Army and become a professional photographer. I saw a chance of putting him and Nigel together to get into all the best and most exclusive parties and fill the column with great words and pictures. Who could say no to the Earl of Lichfield, cousin to Her Majesty the Queen? I told Patrick that, as soon as he was out of the Army, I would pay the rent on a studio he coveted in Kensington for two years on condition I had first call for the *Daily Express* on his photographs. It worked for the *Express*, it worked for me; it worked for Nigel and Patrick, both of whom went on to make their fame and fortune. The first story they covered together was a very swanky do at a stately home to which, of course, Patrick had been invited. He drove through the ornate gates, manned by security men – with Nigel hidden in the boot of his car.

Beaverbrook was a lover of mischief and a lover of journalists. He enjoyed their company. While I usually found it terrifying to meet him, either at his London flat in Arlington House behind the Ritz or down at Cherkley, once I had survived the occasion I realised what a man he was.

Walking through Green Park one day with one of his editors he observed a flock of pigeons pecking at scraps.

'Greedy birds!' he exclaimed. 'Like journalists… Greedy. You must cut down on their expenses.'

I don't think the editor ever did this but, wisely, he agreed with his chairman. On one occasion the Beaver was furious that the *Sunday Times* had stolen a *Daily Express* star and he summoned his then editor, Bob Edwards and his deputy, my old mentor, Harold Keeble, to his villa at Cap d'Antibes on the Riviera.

This anecdote has been told by the subject of it so I feel I am able to repeat it with confidence.

'Who is the best journalist on the *Sunday Times*?' Beaverbrook demanded of Bob. Never slow with an answer Bob replied quickly: 'Smith, Lord Beaverbrook.'

'Then hire Smith,' ordered Beaverbrook.

In the car on their return Keeble asked Bob which journalist he was thinking about.

'No idea,' replied Bob. 'But there is bound to be someone called Smith on their staff!'

Thus Godfrey Smith, to his amazement, was hired by the *Express* at double his *Sunday Times* salary.

5
FEATURING IN FEATURES

From the start I had always been interested in making newspapers and when Bob Edwards, the brilliant and mercurial editor of the *Daily Express*, taken by my record on William Hickey, offered me the post of features editor I turned my back on the glamorous world of gossip and threw myself into a whirlwind sixty-hour week, loving every minute but certainly neglecting my lovely family, by now of four children. They tell me they have forgiven me and I tell them they were never far from my thoughts – both of which are more or less true.

The paper was at that time such a powerful organ that most distinguished writers were happy to contribute, despite Beaverbrook's edict that no feature was to be longer than 20 inches when measured on the galley proofs.

We had on the staff an unmatched array of writers and specialists including the great spy expert Chapman Pincher – always a friend; the highly able Ann Leslie; Trevor Evans; fairly briefly my old Suez mate Michael Parkinson; Barrie Devney; Charles Douglas-Home, son of the former prime minister and later editor of *The Times* and his brother, Robin Douglas-Home; and Percy Hoskins, the king of crime reporters. There were also several of the country's best cartoonists including Osbert

Lancaster, Giles, Michael Cummings and Mel Calman.

To this galaxy we added a column on pop and rock written by one of an up and coming band – George Harrison, whom I had met when we got the Beatles to pose with a set of baby quadruplets we had under contract.

I remember Robin Douglas-Home telling me how, when they visited their father in Coldstream there was an array of old fur coats hanging outside the breakfast room. You put one on before sitting down to eat – or you froze to death! Robin was often at a loss about what to write in his column. That was when my training on the Hickey column came to the rescue and I would sit him down and question him about what he had done and who he had met over the previous week. The result was, I hope, very readable!

A succeeding editor of the *Express*, Derek Marks, decided we should launch a country column on Saturdays and suggested that it be written by Henry Williamson, the *Tarka the Otter* author. Henry agreed on one condition – that the column would be illustrated by an astounding artist called Richard Richardson, who had illustrated several of Henry's books.

Through his publisher I eventually tracked down Richard who was a bird warden on a remote wild life sanctuary owned by the National Trust at Blakeney Point in Norfolk. Long before the age of mobiles he had no phone number of course. So I rang the little post office in Blakeney itself and asked if there was a way of contacting him.

'Oh, the bird man,' said the helpful lady at the other end of the call. 'He comes in here once a week on Tuesdays to pick up his bird seed.'

I decided that I had to go and seek him out so I drove up to Norfolk, got out to Blakeney Point and found 'the bird man' in a fairly basic dwelling.

He was a shy man but was impressed by Henry Williamson's admiration for him so he eventually said he would draw – but how on earth would he get his drawings to Fleet Street? I pointed out that he went to the Post Office once a week. I would send him poste restante, a supply of backed and stamped envelopes and, each week advance notice of which birds, animals or plants Henry was going to write about the following week.

Then came the question of payment.

'Money's no good to me,' he said, 'I don't need money.'

'Well,' I said. 'How about I pay for your weekly supply of bird seed?'

We settled on this and for some two years I received the most exquisite series of drawings with every feather, hair or other detail lovingly and accurately portrayed and Richard got his free bird seed which cost the *Express* a couple of pounds.

Henry had also written a series for us on his experiences in the First World War and he gave me a copy of his book about it – *A Patriot's Progress*. I gave it to my first father-in-law, who had survived

Passchendaele and the Somme. He said it was the most accurate account of those horrors he had ever read and that it brought back the painful memories and emotions of his months in the trenches.

As he was a small man he had been made battalion runner, taking messages from one part of the trenches to other sections. On one such journey he fell into a deep shell hole and, as he was wearing dungarees with shoulder straps found he was sinking down and down and could not struggle out. After some time, when he was almost resigned to suffocation in the mud, someone threw him a rope and pulled him out. He had been there so long that he had severe frost bite so was sent to an advanced field hospital. There the nurses gave him first aid and bandaged his feet. They told him it would be two to three weeks before a doctor could come and look at him. Meanwhile they put three copper pennies in each of his bandaged feet. When he asked why they explained the pennies would stain the bandages yellow and the doctor, as soon as he saw the stains, would suspect gangrene, which is highly contagious. So he would immediately rewind the bandages and send him home. Which probably saved his life.

But back to the *Express*. Derek Marks was settling in as editor in succession to Bob Edwards, who remarkably held the post twice and then went on to edit the *Sunday Mirror* and the *People*. Although Derek was an excellent political journalist, there were vast areas of popular journalism about which he knew very little. But in the Fleet Street custom of drinking he was an expert. His capacity was unrivalled in my experience.

I would occasionally be summoned to lunch with Derek. From the office we would go to El Vino, the popular watering hole in EC4. There we would consume a bottle of Champagne each. Then on to the Boulestan – the restaurant then in Covent Garden – where we would sit at the bar, choosing our food while sipping a Paris goblet of dry sherry which they kept in the fridge for the editor.

At the table two of us would have a bottle of Chablis with our first course, on to one or two bottles of claret with our main course, finishing up with a couple of cognacs and coffee. We would then climb into the editor's chauffeur-driven car for the short journey back to Fleet Street. But we would roll by the *Express* building, stopping at Poppins, the staff's favoured watering-hole at the end of Poppins Court. There Derek would rap on the window of the by-now closed pub and the landlord would open up for us. Over several glasses of port he and Derek would discuss which horses to back in the later races that afternoon.

After that we would stagger back to the office – Derek to drink beef tea and me to ask my deputy to take over and to order a taxi to take me home to a bath and a well-earned rest.

However Derek would continue to work all afternoon until it was time to take supper at home, accompanied by some more claret provided by his loving wife. He would then return to the office, inspect the first edition, make suggestions for improvements and later would stroll over to the Press Club where the barman had been preparing gin sours which Derek would consume until midnight. Derek did this six or seven times a week.

Perhaps not surprisingly he died at the comparatively early age of 54.

Of course national newspapers, in those hot metal days were exclusively black and white, as was television. Our television reporter came to me in early 1967 and said he had been invited by the CEO of Philips, the huge Dutch electronics firm, to go, with a senior executive, to Eindhoven to view their controlled colour TV system prior to its rolling out to the public later that year. We went over to Holland and were fascinated by what we saw – a Dutch priest with white hair, dressed in black, demonstrating his hobby—his collection of tropical fish in a large tank...

Later in the penthouse office of Dr Frits Philips, the CEO, our conversation was interrupted by the roar of a squadron of Dutch Air Force fighter jets zooming by at not much above window height. 'I never mind that,' said Dr Philips. 'After all, each of those fighters contains more than £3 million worth of my equipment.'

I came back convinced that newspapers would have to embrace colour if they were to stay alive in the face of colour television and that the old monotone restrictions, clung to by the print unions, would have to go.

My new obsession with colour led the *Express* to begin an experiment with pre-print colour which was prepared on off-set presses in Peterborough and then shipped to Fleet Street, Manchester and Glasgow to be inserted on the hot metal presses along with our black and white newspaper. Cumbersome, expensive and lacking topicality, this nevertheless made a huge impact with readers and with advertisers.

Colour was, in fact, one of the major factors that eventually led to 'new technology', Wapping, Eddie Shah's *Today* newspaper and the final victory, led by Rupert Murdoch, of the newspaper industry over the cloying blackmail of the old print chapels of Fleet Street which had prevented the adoption of all technological advances in printing.

Had this stranglehold not been broken few newspapers would have survived. Those who criticise Murdoch so severely today tend to forget that he saved their bacon. Today the old Fleet Street chapels have gone, the double payments for shifts undertaken by printers signing on for their shifts as 'Mickey Mouse' have been eradicated.

Today colour printed on the day is the norm. It is available on every page of most national newspapers and most advertisers use it to great effect while the editorial side takes great delight in employing it well.

The blackmail of the old print unions had to be seen to be believed. Jocelyn Stevens, at that time MD at the *Express*, did a deal with the manufacturers of 'J-Cloth' then a new cleaning material on the market. To launch it the idea was that every copy of the broadsheet *Express* would carry a sheet of J-cloth inside it. It would be automatically fed into the paper in the press room on our rotary presses.

As the elasticity of J-cloth and newsprint were not the same it was asking for trouble and chaos ensued. Of course the boys in the press room spotted an opportunity. Looking down Shoe lane from my office I saw streams of them bearing away huge bundles of J-cloths being stuffed into cars and vans. Some set up shops on the back of this free bonanza and the black market in stolen J-cloth made a lot of money for a lot of printers.

My relationships with Jocelyn Stevens, who had been appointed by Sir Max Aitken, Lord Beaverbrook's son, were mercurial. He liked to give editorial advice, but as his only experience had been editing the fashionable but low circulation magazine *Queen*, I did not think his advice was always good.

One spectacular disagreement occurred when he and I argued about the order in which some new royal pictures should appear. I insisted that my choice was the right one... and then added that, as they were in colour and were pre-printed in Peterborough, he could not change the order in any case.

This threw him into a towering rage and, not for the first time, he picked up a fashion writer's typewriter and hurled it at me. I dodged the missile and it crashed through the window behind me and landed in Shoe lane, fortunately missing pedestrians in the often busy street.

Despite this assault we remained on relatively good terms and my wife and I were invited by Charles Forte to join Jocelyn's box at the Arc de Triomphe race meeting in Paris. Jocelyn's companion, Vivien Duffield (her fortune was then estimated to be £400 million), had an interest as her brother Alan Clore, had a horse running. She asked me to place a bet on the Tote for her and handed me a French note worth just £10.

'I never bet more than that on anything,' she said. Wise because the horse did not win.

Around this time I caught wind of a putative order for nine consecutive pages of advertising that the emergent nation of Saudi Arabia was thinking of taking in the *Express* to extol their country and tell the west something about their people. While the income was, of course, welcome I did not think their message would come over well with our readers. So, with the co-operation of the advertising department, I contacted the ambassador and suggested that if we sent a reporter and a photographer to Saudi Arabia to tell our readers what the country was all about – warts and all – the result would be more believable than the puff copy they would put in their adverts and they could space out their nine pages of advertising devoted to selling their exports over nine weeks...

The ambassador, inevitably related to the King, agreed – though he swallowed hard when I said I wanted to send a woman feature writer!

(In fact the photographer, a fair haired young man, had a more torrid time and attracted far more sexual interest than the female writer.)

The resulting series was a penetrating and informative first-class piece of journalism and the Saudis saw its huge value. At a thank-you dinner at their embassy I was presented with a Rolex watch that I wear to this day. Was that a bribe? I think not, as it was after the event and was, I think, a genuine gift from a king who thought I had done him a favour.

The old Beaverbrook sentiment about the Empire and Imperial trade survived the Beaver's demise and, in 1968 I was sent on a mission to write a series of features about the opportunities closer attention to the markets in Australia and New Zealand could bring to Britain. Taking in Fiji as well it was an absorbing trip of about a month and included a brief respite, which was a session with an Aborigine in the bush in the art of boomerang throwing.

On my return I attracted quite a crowd in Richmond Park practising my new found skill – usually to some embarrassment for my four small children.

However one working trip to New South Wales had given me a true insight into the scale of Australia. I had landed in Dubbo, in the heart of New South Wales, in a heavy shower of rain. So rare was that occurrence that the local mayor decided it merited a banquet in the town hall in my honour as 'the bringer of rain'.

Over barons of beef and copious beers I met up with a local sheep farmer who invited me to look over his farm next day. He picked me up in his truck and drove me to a nearby airstrip where his little airplane stood.

'Only way to see my place,' he said as I looked surprised. And as we took off I asked him how big his sheep farm was.

'Well,' he said 'It's more of a ranch than a farm. It is just bigger than the whole of Wales.'

That trip also enabled me to meet up again with Tom Jenkins, my first best man, a friend I had met on the *Sunday Express*, who with his wife Babs had emigrated to Perth to work on the *Western Australian* newspaper and was still living there. It proved to be the last time I saw him, as, alas he died in 2014.

6
MOONSHINE

In 1969 two unconnected events took me to the USA. The first was the announcement that Apollo 11 was going to land men on the moon and that the *Express*'s great rival, the *Daily Mail*, had signed a contract with *Time* magazine for the exclusive first person details of the three astronauts, Neil Armstrong, Buzz Aldrin and Michael Collins.

For this potential scoop the *Mail* had paid out a record sum of, I believe, $250,000 and they intended to use it as a re-launch to capture some of the massive *Express* circulation. My experience with colour led the editor to suggest that we could counter this if I could get the first colour pictures of men of the moon back to the UK in time to beat all the others.

At that time quality colour pictures could not be wired home with any degree of reproductive clarity. Also our bureau in New York was riven by personal jealousies and needed the presence of a senior executive to bring the staff back into order. I was on my way.

I found America a refreshing place to work in. Here Press freedom was enshrined in the First Amendment. Official resistance to journalists asking questions did not exist. Even government civil servants had not developed that morbid closet sense of secrecy that still bestrides the Civil Service in

Britain. In New York through a literary contact I obtained an exclusive interview with Philip Roth, whose best-selling novel *Portnoy's Complaint* had ventured into territory no other major novelist had dared to explore before.

Excitedly I reported my potential scoop to the foreign editor of the *Express* who was then my friend David English and was on my way up-state to see Roth. The interview went well and I filed nearly two thousand words to the *Express*.

I then got an apologetic call from David who told me the editor – Derek Marks – had called for a copy of the book and, as soon as he came across the word 'masturbation ' threw it on the floor shouting it was all 'disgusting and pornographic '.

So my interview did not appear in the *Express* – but it was sold round the world through our syndication service and made me a tidy sum in compensation.

I also had a memorable interview with Harry Belafonte, the *Island in the Sun* star. He was deeply concerned about the remains of the colour bar in the States which was well behind the progress we had made in Britain. Despite his star status he still felt the old prejudices towards him and those like him were still there – even in the theatre and Hollywood.

Apollo 11 fever was beginning to rise and I decided that a visit to Houston and the NASA headquarters was required. I asked who would be in charge of distributing the first colour pictures brought back from the moon by the astronauts and was directed to Bob Depiante, picture editor of an organisation called World Scientific Books Chicago,.

He explained to me the process and I started to plan my route back to the UK after the recovery of the Apollo capsule so we could get the colour pictures out before any of the other British newspapers.

That evening the picture editor took me out with his editor, Sid Buller, for dinner. Sid's favourite eatery was a night club in Houston and we gathered there in convivial mood. The wine flowed and we got to talk about the moon shot. Sid, a bullet headed sturdy American, asked me why I was there and I told him about the rivalry between the *Mail* and the *Express* and the huge sum the *Mail* was paying to obtain the astronauts' personal stories.

Sid was shocked. '*Time* magazine does not have an exclusive on those,' he said. 'They have sold something they don't own outright. My organisation has 50% of those stories. *Time* only has the rights to the other half.'

With growing excitement I asked him if he would sell me the rights to publish in the UK and for how much.

'Reckon it's worth $3,000,' he said.

I pulled my personal American Express cheque book from my pocket and wrote out a cheque for $3,000, telling him I would be round to his office in the morning to check out the contract and pick up the material.

The next day, nursing a hangover, I was given the tapes of the interviews, the full transcripts of what the astronauts had told Sid's scientific correspondent, phone access to the astronauts and the details of the contract with NASA and a contract assigning the UK rights to the *Daily Express*.

Our New York office was connected to London by means of a ticker tape teleprinter which was operated by a specialist – but this was a Saturday and he was off duty. I flew back to New York and went into the office. There I sat at the tickertape and laboriously punched out about ten thousand words, filling the room with miles of white tape with holes in it.

I then phoned David, who had just been promoted to associate editor of the *Daily Express*, told him the whole story and said I thought we should go ahead with the first astronaut's story on Monday before *Time* found out and tried to issue an injunction.

David said he knew *Time*'s chief lawyer and that he had never lost a case.

'He has now,' I said and I told him about the contracts and how water-tight our case would be. I then flicked the send switch and the mound of tape started to feed across the Atlantic while I retired to Costello's, the bar at which we regularly refreshed ourselves.

The *Express* duly ran Neil Armstrong's story on the Monday, Buzz Aldrin's on the Tuesday and Michael Collins's on the Wednesday.

I fancy that the loss of what he had hoped to be the plank on which the *Mail* would come back helped the then Lord Rothermere, who was not very well, to say to his son Vere that he should have a go at reviving the paper.

It was, of course, Vere, who later succeeded to his father's title, who did just that – luring David English away from the *Express*, first (later that same year) to edit the *Daily Sketch*, then two years later as editor of the *Daily Mail* to lay the foundations of a new, tabloid sized newspaper, with a distinct appeal to women as well as men which was to overtake the once mighty *Express* and capture the nation's middle class.

Came the actual moon-shot and I returned to Houston with Ross Mark, our man in Washington, and Richard Kilian an ace reporter from our American staff. The Press interest was strong – more than 3,000 journalists in the NASA Press Centre, with banks of cable machines provided by Western Union.

I looked at them and at the Press gang and decided that, when **the** landing came there would be no way we could get our report back to London within a couple of hours and our editions would be running already at that time. Our New York office had a direct line from there to London and could patch any phone call through. As the landing grew near I dialled New York and for forty minutes the three of us took turns in talking to New York to keep the line open. As soon as the Apollo landed we were patched through to London and began filing our story, taking it in turns to fill in the narrative. London told us we beat all the agencies which gave them a flying start. I have the front page to this day;

MAN IS ON THE MOON

By Robin Esser, Ross Mark and Richard Kilian.

Houston.

I remember staggering out the Press Room in Houston at night after many hours covering the unfolding story and looking up at the moon. I thought then that I would never forget the day we reached out into space and that my grandchildren would be in thrall when I told them about that achievement.

But the job of getting the colour pictures back to the UK was still ahead of me. I learnt that some newspapers and news magazines had hired private jets but I thought they might be delayed by air traffic control in favour of scheduled flights. So, when the precious packet arrived I had hired a motorbike to take me to the airport at Houston and was booked on a direct flight to New York. There I needed to transfer onto a transatlantic flight but they were all full!

I told the girl behind the check-in desk that I had the first colour photos of Apollo Eleven on the moon in my hand and I thought the crew might want to see them.

She looked at me unbelievingly so I showed her one of the pictures from the packet.

'Come with me,' she said and I stepped over the luggage weighing platform and went into the office behind. There the captain and crew of a BA flight were waiting ready to board. I showed them all the pictures I had and they were enthralled and greatly impressed. I explained that I had to get them to the UK quickly so the *Daily Express* could print them.

The captain turned to the purser and said that one passenger they had picked up in the Caribbean on the way up looked to him as if she was over the limit for a pregnant woman to fly. She was turned off the plane for a medical examination and I had her seat. She was allowed to fly on a couple of hours later, so I had no conscience about the matter.

Back home the laborious business of pre-print colour had been streamlined as far as it could and within a very short time the *Daily Express* appeared with a front and back page devoted to the conquest of the moon in glorious hues. Sir Max Aitken, chairman of the Express Newspapers, sent me a hero-gram and I was promoted to associate editor alongside David English.

David and I were family friends, not just work colleagues. We used to go sailing – taking our boats and our families to Holland in the summer, later joined by the third musketeer, Stewart Steven who was originally the *Express* diplomatic correspondent and then succeeded David as foreign editor. Stewart, a highly skilled journalist, went on to edit the *Mail on Sunday* and the *Evening Standard*. I was a great admirer of his talent and when he died prematurely I missed him a great deal.

At one point David and I decided to try to break into television and together we wrote a script for a TV series based on the adventures of a Twiggy like model and a photographer. We came close to getting it commissioned by the BBC but in the end it sank into obscurity though a similar idea was the story of the film *Blow Up*.

It was fairly clear at this juncture that the editor's health might not allow him to continue for long. David and I both felt we had done enough to be in line for the job and we had a private pact that whichever of us got the job the other would work and be a loyal (but useful!) deputy. In the end neither of us was chosen and the management, in their wisdom, chose the editor of our Scottish edition, Ian McColl, to take over.

For David this mattered little as he was already in negotiation with Vere Harmsworth to take over the *Daily Sketch* from where he was to move to the *Daily Mail* to begin the revolution that turned that paper into such a success. However, back in London I was parachuted into the picture department to help the photographic side of the *Express* – rather neglected by Derek Marks – back into the prominent position it had previously enjoyed. This was not difficult as the paper still had an incredible cast of really excellent press photographers, including David Cairns, Bill Lovelace, Stan Meager, and Doug Morrison.

One day news came in of the hijacking of three international passenger liners in the Jordanian desert at Dawson's Field.

I called for Stan Meager. 'Get out there and get me a picture of the three planes with a caravan of camels walking across in the foreground. Get it and I will put it across page one and across the back page.

A few days later Stan got the picture and I did run it across the back and front pages. It was a great piece of journalistic endeavour but it had a sting in the tail. When Stan got back he handed me his eye watering expenses.

'I had to pay for every camel and every camel driver,' he explained. 'And camels are not cheap in Jordan.'

7

NORTH OF WATFORD GAP

For me the change of editorship eventually meant a move back up north as I was soon asked to take over the northern editions of the paper, based in Manchester, where we had a staff of more than 200.

We also covered Ireland and, as this was the start of the big IRA campaign of bombs and violence we led the front page of the national editions more often than not.

My arrival in Manchester coincided with the retirement of the long serving PA to the editor and a hunt for a new one. The Brook Street Bureau was asked to find suitable candidates but as one followed another they did not seem to be able to find the right person.

In exasperation one day I phoned the office to talk to the manageress. After a time I said she sounded like the sort of person I wanted. Why didn't she come and see me?

'But I can't type,' she said.

'I don't need a typist,' I replied. 'I can type. So can everyone else here. I need someone to run my life.'

So Sandy Greig became my PA. Several months later I wandered into her office just outside mine to find another young woman sitting on her desk. Sandy introduced me as the two had been at Edinburgh University and even shared a flat there. She explained that her friend was now the deputy classified advertisement manager on my paper and her name was Tui France.

'I had better take the two of you out to lunch and you can talk about people I don't know and I will pay the bill,' I said. And that is exactly what we did. Little did I know then that, ten years later, a decade after I had become a widower, I would marry that girl and have two more wonderful sons. But that belongs to a later era.

We had an experienced array of journalists in Manchester when I arrived there, including a young man called Paul Dacre who had recently graduated from Leeds University. Now I had known Paul's father. Peter, when I was on the *Sunday Express* as he was a big by-line interviewer and had also been that paper's New York correspondent. I had sent Paul to Belfast to cover the IRA atrocities and he had filed some impressive stuff from that bomb-torn city – reports that were, of course, carried in all the editions of the *Express*. He used to stay at the Europa Hotel in Belfast which still, today, calls itself the most bombed hotel in the world. Eventually as our staff man in Belfast and his family were weary of the danger presented by the terror campaign, I offered Paul the permanent Belfast job as I thought he would be an outstanding reporter of the IRA's vicious and murderous ambitions.

I later found out that he had consulted one of my senior executives to whom he had confessed that, while he was flattered by the Belfast offer, he really wanted to go to Fleet Street. His reasons were two-fold. He wanted to get on the London staff as soon as possible and he wanted to marry a girl who was working in the capital. The executive advised him to put forward the latter reason as he thought the editor (me) was a softie for that sort thing but would be less swayed by the early ambitions of a young journalist.

Of course I recommended Paul to the editor in London. He married the girlfriend and went on to become the most successful newspaper editor of his time which I suppose confirms my earlier judgement and is a tribute to my 'soft heartedness'...

The Manchester United team at the time was managed by the legendary Matt Busby with whom I had a warm relationship. After some time I persuaded Matt to write his autobiography in which, for the first time, he would reveal the agonising details and emotions he suffered in the aftermath of the 1958 plane crash which had decimated his team of the 'Busby Babes'.

With help from Bill Fryer, our star football writer, *Soccer At the Top – My Life in Football* by Sir Matt Busby was published in hardback in 1973. It was serialised in the *Daily Express* and the television commercial for it was shot at Old Trafford with all the stars of the team, including George Best and Bobby Charlton, running up to Busby to congratulate him on the book. I rang the publishers to suggest they sent 5,000 copies to the Red Devils shop at Old Trafford for the forthcoming Derby match with Manchester City and said I could arrange to have it publicised on the tannoy at the ground at half time and full time.

'Five thousand?' said the publisher. 'That's half our print run and we don't have that many left.'

The publisher was clearly not a football fan, did not watch TV commercials and never read the *Daily Express*. The book nevertheless became a best-seller in hardback and paperback.

We also ran a ghosted column by George Best on our sports pages. George was, of course, the first footballer with pop star status, setting a trend that flourishes today. He was also the target of ambitious girls eager to be seen out with him.

Matt Busby urged him to settle down and find a nice girl to marry, so he was shocked when George announced his engagement to Eva Haraldsted a 21-year-old he had briefly met on a pre-season United tour of Denmark.

The romance didn't last long. George broke off the engagement, saying he could not remain faithful, Miss Haraldsted sued him for breach of promise and went public with a kiss and tell article in a Sunday newspaper and George retreated into his shell.

Came the time for his weekly column and he refused to open the door to our sports reporter, who was due to put his thoughts into print. He could not get through to George who had taken the phone off the hook.

I told the reporter to try again.

He returned crestfallen. 'George wouldn't let me in again,' he said. 'He opened the door a couple of inches and gave me these scribbled notes. I don't think they are any good. Nothing about football in them.'

I took the notes and read them. He was right. Nothing about football in them. Instead it was straight from the heart – George on the iniquities of being the subject of a kiss and tell story from a pretty girl and being sued into the bargain.

I started it on page one. It was the best column (and possibly the only one) he ever wrote unaided. It showed how alone he really was and it did a lot to explain his later slide to the depths of alcoholism.

I prefer to remember him at his glorious pinnacle and to recall the warm heartedness that those close to him knew only too well.

I will always remember Matt, being asked what tactics he gave the team at half time in a match, replying: 'Tactics? I just told them all to give the ball to George.'

He also described George as having 'talent in both feet...Sometimes I think he had six feet.'

Later I became friendly with *George* and was occasionally allowed to kick a football around with him on informal training days. Alas I cannot boast of beating him in a tackle. Six feet? – More like eight.

It was in the summer of 1972 that my good luck had run out.

My whole family was involved in a serious road crash in France. Our four children and I were all hospitalised but my wife Shirley tragically did not survive. In his hospital bed in France my first son, Daniel, who received a bad head injury, was thrilled to get a football, organised by George Best and signed by the whole Manchester United team as a get well gesture. It impressed the nurses too and, not surprisingly, Daniel has stayed a United fan to this day.

The aftermath to this crash was painful and traumatic. Sir Max Aitken, then chairman of Beaverbrook newspapers, a war-time fighter pilot ace and a hero, was a man of great compassion. He decreed that I and my four young children would be better off back in London where I had friends and where they had been brought up, rather than in the north.

I returned to Fleet Street as associate editor of the *Express*.

8

TABLOID ERA

Under the dynamic new editorship of David English and the wise and benign chairmanship of Vere Harmsworth the *Daily Mail* had turned tabloid and set out to deliberately encourage its female readership under the inspired advertising banner 'Every Woman Needs her *Daily Mail*'.

Its success was threatening the dominance and circulation of the *Daily Express* and the decision was made to follow suit and produce a tabloid sized *Daily Express*.

Ted Hodgson, the back bench production king of the *Express* in Manchester, had followed me south and he and I sketched out the designs for the new paper on the floor of the editor's office. Ian McColl, who had been brought down to London to take the national helm following a hugely successful spell as editor of our Scottish editions, looked them over and approved.

The stage was set for the big change from broadsheet to tabloid – a change that was eventually to be followed by *The Times*, the *Independent*, and partly by the *Guardian*, in Berliner size. Today among daily national papers only the *Telegraph* and the *Financial Times* stay at the old broadsheet shape and size.

Ted was a remarkable man and a good friend. He had been a Spitfire pilot during the Second

World War and retained his taste for flying as well as sailing. It was his treat, while still in based in Manchester, to cover the annual TT motorbike races in the Isle of Man – an assignment on which he was accompanied by *Express* photographer Victor Blackman – also a keen pilot and the owner of a light aircraft. I would get regular complaints from the police in Douglas, Isle of Man, that landladies had been frightened by a low flying plane which nearly took the chimneys off their roofs. When it was explained that the pilot was probably a war hero who used to fly Spitfires they calmed down and merely issued a warning that it was not to happen again. I knew it would not – at least until next year's TT races.

Back in London the paper was still vibrant and energetic. One of the best stories came about in 1974, when Colin MacKenzie, a reporter on the diary for the *Express* had a tip off that escaped Train Robber Biggs was in Rio de Janeiro and Brian Hitchen, then the news editor, dispatched a team consisting of MacKenzie, photographer Bill Lovelace and reporter Michael O'Flaherty to find him, which they did, and to file an interview with pictures of his life style in Rio.

Editor Ian McColl was very nervous about the story and wanted the police to be informed at once about the probable discovery of a Great Train Robber. Scotland Yard was told as soon as the *Express* team was in the air but the police were delayed by bureaucracy and detective Jack Slipper was not able to arrive until after the paper had secured and printed our scoop.

As usual, when any paper gets a really good exclusive story its media rivals try to knock holes in the tale and to suggest it was obtained in dubious circumstances. There is no greater exponent of this than the BBC.

And the Biggs story brought this out. As I had some media training and the editor was reluctant to appear on TV I was elected spokesman for the paper. The TV crews arrived with yards of cabling at my home in Fulham (it was the weekend) and my children and our Irish setter looked on in amazement at the circus that ensured.

The main accusation was that we had not told the police what we had discovered. I coined the phrase 'parallel inquiries' to explain that we had told them – though we were on our way to Rio before giving the Yard the full picture. Also at that stage, I pointed out, we did not know if Colin's tip-off was true or not and we certainly did not want to let our exclusive out of the bag. In fact the whole row about how and when the *Express* had told the police was pointless because when Jack Slipper arrived soon afterwards he found that Biggs could not be arrested and brought back to Great Britain because Biggs' then girlfriend, Raimunda de Castro, a night club dancer, was pregnant. Brazilian law at the time did not allow the parent of a Brazilian child to be extradited. Subsequently in April 1977 Biggs attended a drinks party on board the British frigate HMS *Danae*, which was in Rio for a courtesy visit, but surprisingly he was not even arrested then while technically on British territory.

Shortly after this time I was invited by the film publicist, Charlie Berman, and film producer Cubby Broccoli – who always claimed the vegetable was named after his family – to go to Thailand to visit the set of the latest Bond film, *The Man With The Golden Gun*. The filming was on the island of Phuket, then a little known resort with only one hotel and a glorious beach overlooked by a towering volcanic rock from which the villain of the piece, Scaramanga, could launch his equipment which would harness the rays of the sun and destroy anything he wished. It was here that the tiny actor Herve Villechaize, who played Scaramanga's evil dwarf accomplice, sidled up to the leggy Swedish Bond girl, Maud Adams and whispered 'I would lurve to make lurve to you'. To which Maud uttered the classic put down of all time: 'If I notice you doing that I will slap you!'

A little later, when Cubby was shooting Ian Fleming's fantasy adventure *Chitty Chitty Bang Bang* I persuaded the producer to let us have the car that Truly Scrumptious – Sally Ann Howes – drove into a river, as a prize in an *Express* competition. Cub 1 was its registration number and it was eventually won by a collector of vintage vehicles.

I had first met Lew Grade, the Ukrainian-born naturalised Brit who dominated early TV in this country, when I was running the William Hickey column. We had remained in touch over the years and when he decided to revive the *Pink Panther* films in 1975 he invited me and some other journalists to accompany him to see the final scenes set in Gstaad, the Swiss resort of fairy tales.

Surrounded by Alps, the town's most prominent feature is a picturesque castle that sits on a hill overlooking the village. At night, the Palace hotel is lit by spotlights and the eaves of every chalet in the village are illuminated by strings of small white lights.

No expense was spared. The plane Lew hired to take the Press crew to Switzerland was painted with images of the Pink Panther and the pavements of the town of Gstaad were decorated with pink foot prints of a panther. We were accommodated in the Palace hotel, the town's most expensive, and wined and dined like millionaires.

Lew was an engaging character. In his early days he had been a professional dancer and he retained his dancing skills for the rest of his life – the Charleston being his favourite.

Lew's interest in producing films was finally cooled with the movie called *Raise the Titanic*. It was so expensive and lost so much money that he observed, wryly,

'It would have been cheaper to have lowered the Atlantic!'

My old good luck remained working for me in the shape of an invitation to join a high-powered delegation from Fleet Street to visit China as the guests of Premier Chou En-Lai. Led by Vere Harmsworth – about to become Lord Rothermere – and including such luminaries as Donald Trelford, soon to be appointed editor of the *Observer*, Peregrine Worsthorne of the *Telegraph*, Patrick Sergeant of the *Mail*, Sir Ted Pickering and his wife Rosemary and Peter Gibbings from the *Guardian* group we spent an amazing three weeks in the country still dominated by its iconic leader Chairman Mao and the extremist Red Guard.

An able diplomat, Chou was largely responsible for the re-establishment of contacts with the West in the early 1970s.

His policy towards the Indo-China area was to neutralise the region and he was alarmed at the prospect of the Viet Cong, backed by the power of Russia, producing a hostile presence in that country on China's southern frontiers. He judged that a long lasting alliance between Vietnam and the USSR was a danger to his country. He was therefore keen to impress on the media in Britain the advantages of solidifying Western Europe by backing the Common Market and thus forming a balancing act in Europe against Russia.

Of course he could not be seen to back Nato as it was regarded at a 'militaristic weapon of imperialism' – but backing an economic institution and the people it might benefit was acceptable in a

81

communist state and to the venerable head of state Chairman Mao.

While we were all aware of the subtleties of this approach we were treated to an extraordinary glimpse of what had been a closed society for many years. One of the high ranking officials delegated to accompany us round the country spoke such good English that I asked where he had practiced it.

I found he had been the jailer of Anthony Grey, the Reuters correspondent who had been sent to China to cover the cultural revolution in the late 60s and ended up being arrested and confined to a 12-ft square whitewashed room in his own house in revenge for the jailing in Hong Kong of eight left-wing journalists for allegedly violating emergency regulations during riots in the crown colony. Through the long hours his jailer practiced his English on his captive. He had also strangled Grey's pet cat in front of Grey at the start, just to prove that he could not be influenced by his prisoner.

We were still in China on the day Saigon fell to the Russian backed Viet Cong – April 30 1975 – and the streets of Peking were alive with celebrations and flag waving on May 1st. Foreign Minister Chiao Kuan-Hua was more restrained. A tall, elegant relaxed man, his Mao uniform was of a superior cut and cloth and white silk socks peeped out under his trousers. He echoed the policy of his premier, Chou En-Lai, recognising that a Vietnam under the influence of Russia was a threat to China and, while he could not be seen to back America, it had become all the more important that a balancing power in Europe was needed to counter the increased Soviet threat. His command of the English language, as he explained this rather tortuous piece of diplomacy to us, was clearly good but he used an interpreter, we thought, to give him time to consider what he was going to say. Nothing like being careful. With quiet exasperation he murmured: 'If only the United States had listened to us twenty years ago.'

Later we were taken to the editorial office of the only newspaper the *People's Daily*. The technology was ancient even by Fleet Street standards – the presses old hot metal ones and many of the bigger headlines were set using wooden blocks. But its audience was vast as it was read out on loud speakers to workers in the rice fields throughout the country.

After a look round the pressroom we were ushered into the editor's office and provided with lots of green tea. Time ticked by. Eventually I asked what the delay was all about.

'An important story for the front page is still not ready. We cannot go to press without it,' we were told.

The completed paper eventually was brought in. I asked which was the vital story that had held up production. They pointed to a panel across the top of page one.

'It is a letter from Chairman Mao congratulating the Malaysian Communist Party on the 25th anniversary of its foundation.'

I refrained from remarking that the story had taken 25 years to reach its maturity. Chairman Mao could do no wrong. His word commanded respect and obedience over the whole of China. Women were allowed to wear only the Mao tunic and trousers in grey – the sole exception was in the theatre where they were allowed a government approved blue dress. The men all wore the same colourless tunic and trousers. Only government officials and VIP visitors like us were driven in cars. The rest of the population walked or rode bicycles.

Shops could not have windows displaying their wares. The capital was nearly birdless. Just a few years before Chairman Mao, hoping to preserve crops, had issued orders that the population had to go outside at dusk and bang bin lids to prevent birds roosting and, when they fluttered to the ground exhausted they must be stamped on. The result was a huge rise in pests and insects and a dramatic increase of flies. The Chairman rescinded the order when it proved his instruction had the opposite effect intended and substituted an order to his 500 million subjects that each and every one of them must kill at least ten flies a day.

While in the capital we all went to the Peking Duck restaurant. It had one section for foreigners and another for Chinese. And the most prized part of the duck was the beak, done to a crisp. I fear I was the one chosen to enjoy it.

The most prized possessions for the Chinese then were a bike, a sewing machine and a radio. These added up to about £85 – approximately three to four months wages for most.

Wherever we went we were entertained by the officials of the local commune who took great delight in trying to drink us (especially the ladies in our party) under the table with constant toasting of their fiery liqueur. Little did they realise that Fleet Street had hardened us all to the booze and generally we left them under their tables.

We were all put on an overnight train to the north of the country to visit a model commune where the ideal communist social group would demonstrate how the strict interpretation of the Marxist doctrine could work. On the train I shared a sleeper cabin with Donald Trelford. I had the top bunk and he had the bottom one. At some point in the middle of the night the train came to a sudden screeching halt and the samovar of green tea the guard had placed on the small table tipped all over Donald, waking him with a start. It was the beginning of a friendship that has lasted to this day.

On our way out of China there was a near diplomatic incident. Vere Harmsworth's wife 'Bubbles' had joined us in Canton for the last two days of our tour. Bubbles was a very determined character who liked to get her own way but I had always got on well with her ever since my gossip column days.

In 1975 there was a gap between China and Hong Kong, the crown colony the Chinese did not officially recognise. So those travelling this route had to disembark from the train on the Chinese side, walk 100 yards across the border and take Hong Kong transport into the port. We all dutifully left our train and trudged across to the Hong Kong side. Then someone looked back to see Bubbles siting on the unused track. She refused to walk 'just because of the silly Chinese'.

'Ask the Governor to bring his limousine as close to the border as it can,' I said, 'and I will go back and talk to her.' I sat next to Bubbles on the rail track and told her the Governor of Hong Kong had come up to the border especially to see her and take her back to civilisation alone, without all these tiresome journalists. This mollified her and she took my arm as we gently strolled across the border and I handed her over to the Governor. Phew.

9

A CHANGE OF DIRECTION

In 1974 the management of the *Daily Express* had decided that yet another new editor was necessary to revive its now flagging circulation. They identified a shortlist of three editors they thought could do the job. They were David English, Larry Lamb and Alastair Burnet. The first was the outstanding editor of another middle market newspaper, the *Daily Mail*, and he was not going to change the job in which he was cherished and for which he was well rewarded. The second was an outstanding editor of a red top – the *Sun* – and there was no way at that stage Murdoch would let him go. The last was the spectacularly successful editor of the *Economist* and anchor-man of News At Ten, ITN's flagship programme.

This shortlist convinced me that those in charge at the *Express* did not know in which direction they wanted to take the paper – down market, up market, or somewhere in the middle market. In the end Alastair, looking for a new challenge, took the chair and I found him a delight to know and work with.

His reputed taste for Scotch never worried me. After Derek Marks he was almost tee-total – but I was unsettled by what I considered was a lack of direction and enthusiasm on the part of those in charge of the company. Success in newspapers only appears to come when a charismatic owner or chairman is partnered by an experienced editor who knows what he or she needs to attract readers to their paper. Think Beaverbrook and Christiansen, Think Larry Lamb and Murdoch, think Andrew Neil and Murdoch, think David English and Vere Harmsworth, think Paul Dacre and the present Lord Rothermere.

Arthur Christiansen was editor when I first joined the *Daily Express* but within weeks he left to be followed by a regiment of leaders – Edward Pickering, Bob Edwards, Roger Wood, Bob Edwards a second time, Ian McColl, Alistair Burnet, Christopher Ward, Larry Lamb, Nicholas Lloyd, Hugh Whittow, to name just a few of them. In fact the *Daily Express* has had 16 editors in the 57 years since Christiansen left. The *Daily Mail* only six.

So, when an offer came along from David English to join Louis Kirby at the *Evening News* to try to re-invigorate London's biggest selling evening paper I jumped at the chance. There is no doubt that I felt even closer to readers on the *News*. The difference between a national newspaper and a community one. We certainly gingered up the features side of the paper with the use of colour and getting the staff motivated.

One of those writers was Trudi Pacter and she was, I believe, the best ever practitioner of the genre of articles nicknamed 'kiss and tell'. She had the remarkable ability to get intimate details of past and sometimes passing romances out of the jilted and translate them into highly readable articles. Trudi was one of our great star writers. She went on to become a successful author of racy novels – and to marry a baronet. She is now a qualified psychotherapist.

Another masterly writer on the staff was Anne de Courcy who produced some wonderful features. She later became one of this country's leading historical authors. And, of course, the editor of the *News* diary, John Blake. Energetic, charismatic, gifted and always up with the latest gossip in town, John afterwards became a hugely successful publisher of books with many a best seller to his name.

Honed by the polished talents of the *News* theatre critic, Felix Barker and illustrator Peter Jackson, we revisited the Seven Wonders of the World in glorious colour (still pre-printed) bringing a welcome splash of sophistication to what was a very good evening newspaper.

Then I received an invitation from the RAF to write a feature about their fighter squadrons in an attempt to stimulate recruitment. I accepted and told them I wanted to fly in one of their most modern planes to get the feel of piloting such a powerful weapon. I duly went for the necessary medicals and, to my astonishment passed them all, so I reported at RAF Coltishall for a boy's own adventure in the co-pilot seat of one of two Jaguar fighters that the force had to train pilots.

As we took off I felt the huge power of the machine which seemed to zoom into the air effortlessly. We flew across England and into Wales, did a dummy bombing raid on a railway tunnel, coming out so steeply we experienced more than 4G, and coming back at a height above the commercial traffic I was allowed to pilot the plane home to East Anglia. Some experience and the resulting piece in the paper proved very popular and certainly impressed my children!

Shortly afterwards it was decided to launch a colour magazine to be given away free with the paper to help boost circulation and I was asked to take over the project.

First though Louis and I were asked to lunch with the chairman – Vere Harmsworth – to hear his ideas about the magazine's contents and looks. We duly went to the Savoy Grill. Over lunch we were treated to an insightful monologue about the part played by the middle class in revolutions round the world. It was masterly and fascinating. As Vere rose to signal the end of lunch I asked about the magazine.

'Oh,' he replied, 'Cartoons. Your magazine needs plenty of good cartoons.'

With that he left. I duly included two pages of good cartoons in the magazine. When the mag appeared it was pretty attractive – so good in fact that the street sellers frequently also gave it away with the rival *Evening Standard* – thus blunting its effectiveness at bolstering the *Evening News*.

The cost of distributing the *Evening News* in the crowded streets of London was crippling, sales were declining despite all our efforts and in 1980 it was decided to merge it with the *Standard*.

This decision was also motivated by Associated's desire to launch a Sunday paper – the *Mail on Sunday*. Their *Sunday Dispatch* had been sold to the *Sunday Express* in 1961. The last issue of the *Evening News* was published on October 31, 1980. The first edition of the *Mail on Sunday* was launched on May 2, 1982.

It was suggested that I might like to take over the group's still successful showbiz magazine, *Weekend*, which for many years had been making a profit, unlike most of its cousins in Associated. The only problem was that its veteran editor, David Hill, had other ideas. He did not see why he should make way for anybody – including me. So, not for the last time, I was out of a job.

A number of us at this point decided to launch a free newspaper for London. I think, in retrospect, though we were pioneers, we were a little before our time. A weekly, publishing on Fridays, the *Free Weekender* was to be printed on the now fairly idle press that Woodrow Wyatt had brought for his Banbury plant to print the defunct *Evening News* magazine. Woodrow was an entertaining character. He invited us and his printers to his house next to Lords cricket ground for a pre- Christmas party.

For this he had carefully removed the best of his furniture and paintings into two big removal vans which were parked in the street outside and he had hired a band made up of several small and elderly Hungarian musicians. Distributing song sheets to us all, he conducted a rousing session of carols from all his guests by waving an enormous Churchillian cigar in the air.

The former advertising manager from the *News*, Richard Caisley, was to look after the advertising side of the *Free Weekender*, and bring in the income. I was to run the editorial side. With a distribution at main commuter outlets by willing students and a great deal of enthusiasm we plunged into publication.

Unfortunately the advertising sales team met considerable resistance from the industry which was, at that time, not convinced about taking space in a free newspaper and still tends always to be rather conservative, while talking boldly about being innovative.

As the weeks went on Caisley tried running free advertisements to encourage others to join in but this did not help our finances. At the same time Woodrow Wyatt's Banbury printing business, suffering from the drag on his resources of the plant he had bought to print the *News* magazine, was in trouble. Woodrow, a long-time friend of Rupert Murdoch, appealed to him for help.

Rupert was interested in the concept of a free newspaper in London – a concept he revived 20 years later with *thelondonpaper*. Alas it was no more successful than ours although it had huge financial resources compared with ours. Rupert lent us one of his financial executives – who later proved a broken reed – and made some very useful editorial suggestions to me. To no avail. When the whole enterprise came crashing down Murdoch also took upon himself the task of paying our journalists what they were owed. I was left with a big bill for the remainder of our lease on the building we had rented near the British Museum and Richard Caisley disappeared to Canada, leaving me to pick up the pieces.

You live and learn. But luck did not desert me and another super job was round the corner.

10

EXPRESS ON SATURDAY

One day in 1981 I got a call from Christopher Ward who had recently been appointed editor of the *Daily Express*. Christopher was an extremely popular journalist with the *Daily Mirror* when I first met his sister Cherry on the *Sunday Express*. Through her we had met and we had kept in touch over the years. Now he had a project he wanted me to run. Actually he and his managing director, the effervescent Jocelyn Stevens, had first thought of my old mentor Harold Keeble for the job but Harold had reached the end of his career and had recently and tragically died. So it had to be me. I was handed the contract at Harold's funeral in Golders Green.

Christopher's idea was to run a personality, life-style, entertainment section on Saturday in the *Express*. This was a revolutionary idea as up to then Saturday papers had been dull unless you were interested in gardening or staying at a boarding house in the West Country – both activities being the main content of the classified advertisements that support the end-of-the-week issues.

But Christopher was among the first to see that the advent of Sunday shopping was going to make the Saturday papers much more interesting for display advertising and that, in response, the papers published on that day would have to be more stylish, more attractive and edited with the aspirations of their readers in the forefront of the mind.

As the rival *Daily Mail* had just launched its new Sunday paper, Christopher had decided to call his weekend magazine section *Express on Saturday* as a cheeky sort of gesture towards the *Mail on Sunday*. We brought in the novelist and happy imbiber Kingsley Amis to write a drinks column. We brought in Bevis Hillier to write an antiques column, we brought in Richard Compton Miller to write a gossip column about people and we called upon the hugely table *Express* team of feature writers to provide us with sharply written and incisive articles. *Express on Saturday* was a pioneering section in daily paper terms and the predecessor of many other similar efforts by Fleet Street to adapt to Britain's new take on the weekend.

It also brought me back to the group on which I had started. Back then it was owned by Lord Beaverbrook. It was now owned by Trafalgar House, whose senior partner was Victor Matthews, a successful builder and one of the powerful figures at the firm that also owned Cunard, the international shipping company. They paid just £13 million for the business. Having achieved his peerage as the reward for becoming a newspaper owner Lord Matthews devoted as much time to his favourite pastime of horse racing as he did to his paper.

Recently Christopher, who has remained a firm friend, told me that he was called to Matthews' office to discuss the falling circulation of the paper and how it could be reversed. All Matthews said was: 'If it falls below 2 million I'll fire you.'

When that happened Christopher went on to found Redwood, a firm that specialised in creating magazines for companies such as Marks & Spencer and Sky TV. He eventually became a millionaire through this. So there was an ultimate consolation in his firing.

He also went on to write a best-selling book about the sinking of the *Titanic*. Remarkably his grandfather was a violinist on board the doomed liner and part of the band that played on as the great ship sank below the waves. Unknown to his grandfather, who perished in the icy waters, his fiancée, who was waiting for him to return, was pregnant and eventually gave birth to Christopher's mother. His best-selling book, *And the Band Played On*, is a first-rate analysis of the aftermath of that great sea tragedy and is a tribute to Christopher's abilities as a researcher and a writer.

As I have said, impatient for success in the face of the rising strength of the *Daily Mail* under David English and Vere Rothermere the *Express* fell back on the usual knee jerk reaction all failing media groups seem to employ – as Matthews had promised, they changed the editor. This time it was Sir Larry Lamb who took the poisoned chalice. Larry was, of course the architect, with Rupert Murdoch, of the soaraway *Sun*. However, the enthusiastic and coffer-filled backing was lacking and, expert journalist that Larry still was, there was little he could do on his own to stem the ebbing tide of readers. I found it a privilege to work alongside Larry, who still retained much of the sparkle and attack that had brought success to the *Sun*.

He took me back into the mainstream of the paper, making me an associate editor – in effect his number three. In fact the only argument we ever had was about the merits of Louis Roederer Crystal champagne against Krug and we would occasionally repair to a bar to continue the discussion. But the stress of working with a management with few resources and even less understanding of what it took to create a successful mass circulation newspaper I am sure contributed to a major heart attack. Larry was fortunate that this happened in his office at the *Express* and his quick-thinking deputy, Leith McGrandle, called the emergency services and got him into St Bart's hospital before too much damage was done.

While Larry was recovering the *Daily Express* was run by Leith and me as stand-in deputy. Often I was editing on a Sunday and I frequently took calls from Peter Walker, at that time Margaret Thatcher's energy minister and chief plotter for the government against the miners' strike led by the militant Arthur Scargill.

Walker was a clever operator – as indeed befitted the man, who, with Jim Slater, was the father of a business that bestrode the buying and selling of shares in all the major companies and corporations – and he was aware that newspapers, sometimes short of news on a Sunday, would often be grateful for a steer about the conflict that their political editors could turn into story, even a front page lead, on a quiet day.

Eventually I invited Walker to lunch at the Savoy Grill. In conversation at the bar beforehand we were chatting about the differences between government and private sector work and he told me that the best thing Edward Heath had ever done for him when he joined the cabinet was to make him sell his huge portfolio of shares.

'I invested much of it in wine,' he told me. 'It has done rather better than the shares did – and it has meant I have drunk fine wines ever since. I just ring my wine broker and he sends me a case or two which hardly dents my stock.'

When we sat at the table I am afraid my eye slid down the wine list to the choicer suggestions at the higher prices. Well I couldn't let the side down and the Lynch-Bages was delicious.

Victor Matthews was not in newspapers for the long term. As group managing director and deputy chairman of Trafalgar House, a construction company, he had persuaded the firm to buy Beaverbrook Newspapers in 1977. In 1980 he got his peerage and three years later he sold the newspapers to United Newspapers whose chairman was David Stevens and editorial adviser Gordon Linacre – a man with extensive experience of regional papers in the north of England but limited knowledge of Fleet Street.

Larry Lamb, not in the best of health after his heart attack, decided he had had enough and gave way to Nicholas Lloyd as *Daily Express* editor. Shortly afterwards David Stevens decided it was time the veteran editor of the *Sunday Express*, John Junor, stepped down and he asked me to take over. John was to continue his popular column but he moved from the *Sunday Express* offices to United's headquarters a few hundred yards away from the Black Lubyanka.

Many of John's staff had grown into maturity along with their editor and I arranged terms much better than the gold watch they might have received on reaching 65 for those who wished to retire. All but one were grateful for the consideration I had given them.

As my deputy I appointed Brian Hitchen, a thoroughly experienced and tough professional journalist with whom I had worked in the past. Tragically Brian and his wonderful Irish wife Nelli were both mown down when crossing the road near Alicante in Spain, where they had an apartment. Nelli died on the spot and Brian, who was rushed to hospital, died the next day aged 76.

Unusually, the owner of *Express* newspapers declined to contribute cash for Brian's memorial service at the Fleet Street church of St Bride even though Brian had edited two of the *Express* group's titles. Other newspapers chipped in and it was a memorable send off for a giant of our trade. I miss them both greatly. Brian had an unsurpassed nose for news which was something the *Sunday Express* seemed to have forgotten about.

He identified Henry MacRory – later a much respected senior press officer at Number Ten, and then at the Conservative party headquarters – as the right man to become my news editor and we proceeded to resurrect the news agenda. Ironically it was the newspaper's first world scoop in living memory that first showed up the differences in my ambitions for the paper and those of the chairman. But more of that anon.

A Sunday newspaper is more just a newspaper. These days it consists of many sections but in the mid-80s the profession was only just awakened to this. The *Mail on Sunday*, edited by the hugely able Stewart Steven, clearly had the faith and the investment needed to make it successful. I struggled to squeeze much support out of United. One thing I was able to do was to change our magazine. The editor of it had resigned which gave me the opportunity to appoint the most successful and charismatic features journalist I knew – Dee Nolan, an Australian of huge talent.

Dee, who went on to turn *YOU* magazine into the success it remains today, was working on the features side of the *Daily Mirror* and she jumped at the chance to raise the game of the *Sunday Express* magazine and appeal in a stronger way to our female readership. But first she had to pass a hurdle. Gordon Linacre needed to be convinced she was the right person for the job. They met in my office on a

Saturday morning. After two hours of talking Dee, to my relief, suggested that they ought to leave me to edit my newspaper.

'Yes,' I said. 'Gordon, why don't you take Dee to lunch and you can finish your discussions then.'

Off they went. About 7.30 that evening I got a call on the back bench as we were discussing the content of page one. It was Dee.

'I have just got rid of him,' she said. 'He talked on and on – for the last hour and a half sitting in his car outside my flat. But he seemed to think I can do the job.' Gordon was such a talker that his wife used to ban him from the house and send him down the garden to use his mobile telephone from the potting shed.

I was persuaded by our remarkably able literary editor, Graham Lord, to start a Book of the Year contest. Part of the thinking was that the Booker prize had thrown up some works of literature that were almost unreadable and that our audience not only read but also bought books on a regular basis. The judging panel for our launch year in 1987 included Auberon Waugh (Evelyn's son), Hammond Innes and Monica Dickens as well as Graham and myself.

Worth £20,000 for the winner and £1,000 for each of the five shortlisted authors, it was the most lucrative fiction prize in Britain at the time. The first winner in 1987 was Brian Moore with his novel *The Colour Of Blood*. Alas the book prize was abandoned later on, after I had left, in a cost-cutting exercise.

Such unimaginative management has reduced the circulation of the *Sunday Express* to a measly 600,000 on a good day.

I had always been a cricket fan – difficult not to be if you were brought up in Yorkshire – and as the boss of the *Sunday Express* I found myself in charge of one of my boyhood heroes, Denis Compton, who was still writing for the paper about cricket. My good friend and highly gifted sports editor, Ken Lawrence, came to me one day and pointed out that Denis had a significant birthday approaching and that he had always wanted to be at the Masters Golf tournament to watch the battle for the green blazer.

It was with enormous pleasure that I presented Denis with the tickets to fly to Augusta and report the event, alongside our regular golfing correspondent, for the paper. On his return Ken and I took Denis and his long time Australian mate, Keith Miller, to lunch to celebrate his 70th birthday at Green's in St James's , the restaurant owned by Simon Parker Bowles. The majority of customers that day came over and wished Denis a happy birthday. I could hardly believe I was there.

Our advertising agency for the *Sunday Express* was Dorlands, headed by the clever and hugely successful Michael Bungey, who made a decent fortune during the high days of the advertising industry. Our motoring correspondent, David Benson, and I had the idea of producing a part-work magazine which would feature picturesque routes all over the country for our readers to enjoy at the weekend in their cars. Based on advice from the AA this was a promising initiative – but the management of the *Express* refused to give it their full financial backing. Michael Bungey persuaded one of his most important clients – the British Motor Company, later Leyland – to back it to the hilt taking all the advertising space. I then got a grudging go-ahead from management and the part work proved a big success, adding many thousands to our circulation. Despite this the chairman and his board did not see that the way forward was for investment in the Sunday paper with extra sections and he ignored the recommendations from Michael at our advertising agency and from me to promote the *Sunday Express* against the emergent rival, the *Mail on Sunday*. He used to boast to Vere Harmsworth that his shares were stronger than those of the *Mail* newspaper company. That was the extent of his interest in the business of publishing newspapers.

During my editorship of the Sunday paper I had several meetings with the Prime Minister, Margaret Thatcher – including an invitation to join her at the Chequers along with my wife. The lunch that day was an extraordinary event. It was given to mark the visit to Great Britain of Benazir Bhutto, who was later tragically assassinated in her home country of Pakistan.

Benazir had, like Margaret, been to Oxford and this gave the Prime Minister an idea to find out how many of her guests had also been to that ancient seat of learning.

'Hands up all those who went to Oxford,' she called out. A good number, including myself, raised our hands.

'Now Cambridge,' she said. A few hands went into the air.

'A win for Oxford,' she said. A lone hand went up in the air.

'What about Aberdeen?' enquired Sandy Gall. No one else volunteered.

My relationship with Margaret Thatcher was always above board. Indeed I was a great admirer of her sincerity and her determination to say and do what she meant. Such communication between a prime minister and a Fleet Street editor is entirely proper and part of the democratic process. I certainly never asked Margaret for any favours and she was far more interested in what my readers thought of her policies.

I did tell her that the proposed poll tax was not going down well. She responded that it was totally 'fair'. I thought she was probably right but told her that it would be the most unpopular thing she had ever espoused. And so it proved.

Surrounded by yes men and a few women, it was not difficult to see why she thought she was always right and not difficult to see why my old university chum, Michael Heseltine and other prominent Tories felt it was time she stepped down. It was a cruel let down and no wonder she wept bitter tears when forced to go. We have not seen a Prime Minister as sincere and as able to make positive changes since that day. She hauled Britain out of the grave and on to the international stage.

There was a jolly incident when I, along with several captains of industry, was invited by our advertising agency to fly to Monaco to see the Grand Prix. Ever hospitable the agency took us all out to a luxurious lunch of lobster bouillabaisse with Laurent Perrier rosé champagne at Chez Tetou, a beach side restaurant in San Juan Les Pins. When the enormous bill finally came the agency man in charge of the company American Express card waved it at the maître d'hôtel. Drawing himself to his full height he said *'Pas du plastic!'* Consternation all round as a dozen of us searched our pockets coming up with only some small change in francs.

Now I had, with the arrival of cards, long since swapped the Post Office bank book I used to carry but I still had my cheque book. I took it out, explained it was my personal account in Yorkshire and offered to settle the bill with a cheque.

'Parfait,' cried the maître d'.

The agency was, of course, mortified that their guest had to get them out of a hole. The employee with the useless credit card got on the phone to his London office and ordered them to draw a large sum of cash equivalent to our bill, hire a car and drive it to my bank in Bradford before my cheque reached my account. Honour was saved!

Advertising agencies in those halcyon times often ran special days for their clients – an evening at the opera, a day out shooting game birds, a day sailing.

On one such we were cruising in the Solent in the sunshine when one of the clients asked Michael: 'This is a nice sailing day but does Dorlands ever have a working day'?' It was a joke and taken that way.

The *Sunday Express* was still a broadsheet then and the presses on which we printed could not regularly produce more than 36 pages at a time. It was therefore quite a surprise when the chairman, David Stevens, then ennobled as Lord Stevens of Ludgate, said to me that he thought I should make the *Sunday Express* more like the *Sunday Times*.

I pointed out that the *Sunday Times* could produce 128 pages for its main paper and had several magazines while I had 36 pages and one magazine. I did not convince the chairman who thought he was always right and when, after I left, he had his way and appointed an editor from the *Sunday Times* stable the circulation went into a steep downward spiral.

Before that traumatic time I decided that we should use the impact of our large front page to the maximum effect. When the *Herald of Free Enterprise* ferry sank in Zeebrugge, killing 193 passengers and crew, I splashed a huge picture of the stricken boat on its side and put a circle on the open car port doors. I knew exactly what had happened as I had sailed several times as a guest on the bridge of car ferries crossing the Channel.

The inquiry a year or so later confirmed what the *Sunday Express* had told its readers that day – that the ro-ro ship had left port with its car compartment doors open and had taken so much water on board that it rolled on its side and sank.

But our biggest scoop was to come. We had on our staff a really good reporter called Alfie Lee who was Chinese in origin and whose brother still lived in Beijing (formerly Peking) in a flat near Tiananmen Square.

One Saturday Alfie came to us with the news that the Chinese government had executed one of the student leaders of the Tiananmen demonstration and it was the boy who had held up a tank sent to crush the demo. That picture had gone round the world at the time as a symbol of the opposition of the students to the despotic behaviour of the regime which suppressed all freedoms of its people. 'The tank man' as he had become known had disappeared and now it seemed had been executed.

Knowing how Alfie got his information and how reliable it was I decided to lead the *Sunday Express* on this sensational scoop. You might have thought this would please the chairman. You would be wrong.

He rang me at home on the Sunday and angrily asked why I was leading the paper with 'lies and nonsense'.

'Because I believe the story is true,' I replied.

'It is not. I know the Chinese better than you and they do not do this sort of thing,' he raged.

'I realise you spent some time in Hong Kong as a young man,' I said, not very diplomatically. 'But I did not understand you were close to the present Chinese politbureau. I still believe the story to be accurate.'

'We will talk about this next week,' he said ominously and put the phone down.

I was, of course, nervous but I had trust in my news team and in Alfie Lee. The days ticked by that week with no further calls from the chairman. Then, on the Wednesday evening, three days after our publication on the previous Sunday, the CIA issued a statement saying they had evidence that this young student had indeed been executed in the Chinese capital. Nearly every newspaper round the world led on the story.

Thursday passed still with no call from the chairman. Friday morning passed in silence. On Friday afternoon I called him.

'I suppose you want me to apologize,' he snapped. 'Not at all, chairman,' I said.

'What then?'

'I was hoping you would issue a statement congratulating the *Sunday Express* and its staff on the first world scoop we have had for many, many years,' I said.

'I don't do that sort of thing,' he said.

That response convinced me that I and my chairman were on different planets – and, as I observed before, success only comes to an editor if he has the enthusiastic backing in terms of investment and encouragement from the management.

The final straw came when the *Marchioness*, a river passenger boat, sank right in front of the *Sunday Express* windows overlooking the Thames. I was not in the office that week and the paper was in charge of my wonderful deputy, Charles Garside who had succeeded Brian Hitchen.

Recognising the tragedy for what it was – an important and terrible loss of life – Charles re-plated the *Sunday Express* after the main edition had gone to bed and printed several thousand copies to be distributed in the greater London area. The only reaction we got from management the following week was a grumble that we had put them to the expense of buying extra newsprint!

What a let -down. And a far cry from the days when Christiansen re-plated the *Express* with the R101 airship accident which made his reputation and led to him becoming editor. Chairmen often get their way and, after we parted by mutual consent, Lord Stevens, as I have said, appointed a successor who came from the *Sunday Times*.

My recollection is that he lost over half a million circulation during his tenure which lasted short of two years. But then he probably got even less support from his management than I did. He certainly did not get 128 pages to print or two extra magazines. Charles Garside also left to edit the *European* newspaper, under the controversial ownership of Robert Maxwell, and then go on to buy and run, very successfully, the Miller Howe, a beautiful hotel with stunning views from the banks of Lake Windermere, before returning to Fleet Street as assistant editor of the *Daily Mail*.

It was during my editorship of the *Sunday Express* that the mass exodus from Fleet Street, driven by the need to operate on bigger presses with more colour, the new demands of electronic publishing and Rupert Murdoch's successful ending of the stranglehold of the print unions over the newspaper business, took place. At the beginning of my spell running the *Sunday Express* I was on the top floor of the Black Lubyanka. But there was not room in the cellars of Fleet Street to accommodate the extensive new presses that were replacing the old rotary hot metal presses. So the old building was sold off and we moved to new premises with our print being undertaken in docklands. Thus when I departed the Sunday paper I left a building in Southwark on the south bank of the Thames.

From one senior figure in management I got unstinting and wonderful support. Murdoch Maclennan was the production manager for the group and his help in dealing with the changing technicalities of production was invaluable. He was present every Saturday during my editorship and our friendship has survived down the years as we both changed jobs. He is now the successful chief executive of the Telegraph Media Group. But I shall never forget his support of my editorship when at a board meeting called to discuss my future and my successor and our many social engagements I have enjoyed since.

The changes in the way newspapers were printed were only the start of a revolution the effects of which are still not over. Where it will end is still the subject of mass debate and I certainly cannot foretell the future.

Print may survive, reading a newspaper on an electronic tablet will grow, the on line versions of newspapers are here to stay and are garnering increasing audiences across the world. Social networking sites are particularly active in those countries that do not have a free and unfettered Press as the events of 2011 in the Middle East showed so dramatically.

The contrast between the established media and the unregulated internet becomes more and more obvious. In an age where celebrities take out 'super injunctions' to gag the media but their names are readily available on the internet the imbalance is clear.

The world-wide publication on the internet at the end of 2012 of the pictures of Prince Harry, larking naked in his Las Vegas suite with a bunch of girls and then the pictures of the Duchess of Cambridge topless while sunbathing in the privacy of a villa in the south of France owned by her husband's cousin, Viscount Linley, showed just how the global media is free and demonstrated to the public, but not alas to Lord Justice Leveson, just how like King Canute he was in trying to stem the tide of free expression from sweeping onto the shores of Great Britain. None of his recommendations covered Twitter or

Facebook because, world-wide, they are unregulated and probably unregulatable.

The exercise of contempt of court proceedings against printed and televised media which give too much information about those accused of crimes in court while all their past history is available on the internet is, frankly, absurd. Judges' directions to juries not to look up the internet while sitting on a case is equally swimming against the tide and is merely an invitation for those jurors who are curious to call up Google – if necessary the American version which still contains all relevant information.

11

CROSSING THE RUBICON

Many established journalists on the *Express*, weary of the chopping and changing of ownership, management and lack of direction, migrated to the *Daily Mail* which was, with its Sunday paper, beginning to dominate the so called middle market that had once been the preserve of Beaverbrook's *Daily* and *Sunday Express*. As I departed from the *Express* my predecessor, the loyally-followed John Junor, also left and joined the *Mail on Sunday*. He decided that, following my departure, a new editor from outside would not understand the ethos and the 'household gods' that had made the *Sunday Express* so much a part of middle England.

How right he was. With his column, which he had been happy to write for me as editor, went many hundreds of readers. And my successor could not stem a steep downwards curve in the paper's circulation figures. When John's daughter Penny was writing her warts-and-all biography of Junor she asked me what it was like to become his editor – expecting, I think, a very critical response. She was surprised when I said he had been completely professional, always altering items which I felt were unwise. That, of course, had not stopped him from plotting to replace me. This I know from a first -hand source. Charles Wilson, then the editor of *The Times*, was approached by Junor to edit the *Sunday Express* while I was in charge. When Charlie laughed at the idea of exchanging *The Times* for the *Sunday Express* Junor was quite shocked and taken aback. In his view the *Sunday Express* was a superior paper to *The Times*. Only in circulation terms, I fear.

David English, at the helm of the *Mail*, had always liked the various magazines I had edited and, once I was free of the *Express* group he asked me to produce a magazine to accompany the *Mail* sponsorship of the Motor Show and a pilot colour magazine that was planned to be published with the *Daily Mail* on a monthly basis, hopefully rising to a weekly publication. This was an exciting project and I added to the *Mail*'s esteemed motoring correspondent, Michael Kemp, a team of production and motor writing freelances. Although he did not contribute to the magazine at that time Jeremy Clarkson was still working with that group and we shared a few planning beers in the White Horse on Parson's Green – locally known as the Sloaney Pony. The motoring magazine was a success, complementing the *Mail* sponsorship and enhancing the paper's circulation on its day of publication.

The story of the colour supplement, which we called *Etc* was ultimately less happy. While we produced a classy high glossy production which promised well and was well within budget it coincided with a sudden dip in colour advertising and it was decided it would not be economical to go on producing it.

However it did give me the chance to visit the renowned Chateau Mouton Rothschild in the Medoc, meet the remarkable daughter of the Baron de Rothschild, Philippine, and sample a bottle of the outstanding 1945 Bordeaux while dining with her on the terrace of the Chateau. Philippine's father escaped France to join De Gaulle fighting with the Free French. Her mother was arrested by the Gestapo and deported to Ravensbruck where she died in 1945. Philippine herself narrowly escaped death at the time. She was one of the most charming and forceful women I have ever met and also so full of energy.

There is a story about her father which is not denied. He was due to host a parliamentary delegation from Westminster at the Chateau Mouton. When he heard the delegation had arranged to go for a pre-lunch drink at the Chateau Lafitte he was furious. 'Their palates will be ruined there,' he raged. 'We will serve them curry for lunch!' And he did.

Philippine pursued a distinguished career in the theatre with the *Comedie Francaise* until she joined the family business. It was she who devised the exhibition of paintings for the labels of the Mouton Rothschild wines which had been commissioned by her father since 1945.

Following the decision not to proceed with a regular colour magazine David English asked me in 1990 to launch and oversee a magazine-style section to be published in the main paper every Friday.

Originally called Friday's People, it majored on show business stories and personalities and, although it has changed its name two or three times, it is still running some twenty years later. For the opening day we bought a stunning set of pictures of Hollywood star Jack Nicholson with his baby girl from the photographer Harry Benson – the very same man I had been with at Raymond's Revue Bar all those years ago on the *Daily Sketch* and who was now in the middle of a very successful career in America,

There was a surprising sequel to his pictures of Nicholson. My first daughter, Sarah-Jane, at that time lived in Hong Kong, working with a company that built and refurbished hotels in the Far East. My wife and I went out to visit her and she arranged to take us and a bunch of friends out on a junk for dinner on a small island in the harbour.

One of the friends was introduced to me as 'Harry the helicopter pilot'. On our way back, emboldened by the wine, Harry came up to me and confessed he was worried about a large sum of money he had received from the *Daily Mail*.

Some time back he had rung his old friend Nigel Dempster from the Philippines with some news about a disturbance there and Dempster had put him over to the Foreign Desk. The story ran in the *Mail* and Harry got a cheque for £600. But a few months later another cheque for £10,000 arrived. He was worried about it, had banked it some time ago – but not yet spent all of it.

'Could it have been syndication?' he asked me. It seemed very unlikely.

In the meantime I had gathered that Harry the helicopter pilot was the son of an old colleague, Charlie Benson, 'The Scout' – racing tipster and sports correspondent on the *Daily Express*. So he was a Harry Benson too. 'Tell me, I asked 'did you get the cheque in the first week of November a year or two ago?' He looked nervously at me. 'Yes, how did you know?'

'I started the *Mail*'s Friday's People in October and bought a great set of pictures from a cameraman called Harry Benson,' I said. 'Accounts must have picked the wrong Harry Benson as you were on the books having been paid for the Philippines story.'

'Oh! My god,' he said. 'Will I have to pay it back? I've spent some of it. And will the photographer have missed out on his payment?'

'I will see when I get back,' I said, 'But one thing I am sure about. The other Harry Benson will have been paid. He would not miss out on that. His wife is also his business manager and she will have made sure the money was credited to him.'

In fact as it turned out on my return I was right but the editor decided that, as the mistake was the *Mail*'s and it had all happened some time back no request would go to Harry the helicopter pilot to return the money.

A week later I bumped into Harry's father Charlie at a *Sunday Times* party and told him the story. He roared with laughter and said he would get his son to buy him a slap up dinner next time he was in England.

Joining my team on Friday's People was one of the most able and energetic journalists I have ever met – Martin Clarke. Martin went on to have a hugely successful career and is currently the publisher and editor of Mail Online – the world's most popular newspaper online site. He is a professional journalist of the old school and has an unerring sense of what his readers like and want.

After launching Friday's People with me he went on to help launch the Scottish *Daily Mail*, then *Ireland on Sunday*, then *Standard Lite* – the free London evening, then *Live*, the first name of a magazine designed to appeal to male readers for the *Mail on Sunday*. Today the combined daily readership of the *Mail* print paper, the *Mail* on tablet and MailOnLine is twenty and a half million – surely a world record.

I also employed two skilled journalists who have remained friends to this day. John Clare, who had been a producer of the News At Ten on ITV, had then joined the ultimately unsuccessful New Era TV station founded by the *Mail*, joined me for a productive spell on Friday's People. He ultimately left to found Lion's Den which specialises in presenting medical innovation and drugs for the pharmaceutical industry. He was succeeded by Jon Underwood, not only an accomplished journalist but a keen scratch golfer. His wife is Australian and they decided to return to that country where, after several jobs in the TV industry Jon landed the position of editor of the very successful *Golf Vacations* magazine, enabling him to tour some of the world's most attractive golf courses and play on them – which only goes to show there are some dream jobs in the world that deserving people sometimes land.

As I was a consultant at the *Mail* I was also free to undertake other work and the most fascinating was to produce a magazine to celebrate the 100 years of the women's singles championship at Wimbledon. Along with a gifted young designer, Nick Hopkins, we went to see the board of the All England Club. They promised us advertising revenue from their main sponsors, the help of their museum and its curator but otherwise had no particular editorial requirements and appeared 'relaxed' about the budget. Their only worry seemed to be that they could only communicate with Nick by mobile telephone, which to them, at that time was new-fangled and suspiciously modern! A flexible budget – manna from heaven for any editor.

The first women's singles championship was contested in 1884 between sisters Maud and Lillian Watson, the daughters of a vicar who had a tennis court in his garden. Maud won. As there were no women's singles championships during the two World Wars the 100th was to be staged in 1993. I told Wimbledon that I wanted to produce a gatefold for the magazine – which was to be called *Centre Court* – featuring every woman champion, which would begin in sepia tone or black and white and end in glorious colour. But I warned that production would be expensive. 'We don't mind the cost,' they said. 'But you can't do it. There is only a woodcut of the first match and no photograph of Maud Watson.'

However I found one, much to their delight, as Maud had been invited back to the All England Club for the visit of Queen Mary to mark their silver jubilee and there she was – in comparatively up-to-date tennis kit for then, rather than the long skirts both sisters had worn in 1884. The photograph is now in the Wimbledon museum. That was one of the most enjoyable magazines I edited as I love tennis and I had free access to every court on every day of the championships. The hundredth singles was won by Stephie Graff – a worthy champion on a significant anniversary.

Back at the *Mail* I enjoyed running a lively Friday section which concentrated on the entertainment sector and kicked off with the show business column by Baz Bamigboye and ended with the theatre column by the late Jack Tinker. I used to call them my book ends. Jack was a highly amusing and clever raconteur and these two great friends brought much fun, lightness and brightness into the newspaper and to me. They specialised at parties in a dancing and singing duet – after which Jack would sniffily complain about Baz's dancing.

'You would think, with his background, he would have an innate sense of rhythm,' he would say.

Everyone, but especially Baz, would take that in good humour. I was ably supported not only by those I have mentioned, Martin, John, and Jon but also by a team that included Alan Reed, Rona Johnson, and Susie Hans Hamilton.

When Paul Dacre took over from David English as editor in 1993 he soon asked me if I would swap my direct editorial responsibilities and take up a more managerial role, dealing with industry relations, matters arising from the self-regulation from the Press Complaints Commission, editorial budgets and sundry other issues involving readers, which are part of a daily newspaper office.

I had had a good run on the editorial side and, with the thought accepted that I could keep my hand in by writing the occasional article for the travel editor I agreed. Since freedom of the media is something I have always held dear I was happy to undertake this new role – particularly as I had known Paul for so many years and we had, I think, a mutual respect for each other.

Little did I know what I was letting myself in for but it has been incredibly interesting to work alongside Paul. He is certainly one of the best editors Fleet Street has thrown up since the end of the Second World War. He has an uncanny ability to know what the readers want to read in the next day's paper and he has huge energy to see that it gets there. He pushed the circulation of the paper up to outstrip David English's achievements and he has maintained that core circulation better than the rest of our national newspapers in the face of the fierce competition from the other titles and from the online versions of the paper.

He is also very brave. His exposure of the murderers of Stephen Lawrence in which he named them on Page One of the *Mail* and invited them to sue was a fine example of this. He was equally bravely backed in this by Eddie Young, the *Mail*'s wise and skilful chief lawyer at that time, one of the most understanding and humane lawyers I have ever met. I treasure his friendship.

Paul has a reputation for being a hard editor to please but that is merely a measure of his professionalism. He has a reputation for swearing at his staff. Again that is merely a measure of his determination to get the best out of them for his readers. And he, of course, is the first to see that the backing he gets from the management and from his chairman, the present Lord Rothermere, underpins all his success. His ability to attract the best stars of Fleet Street and to maintain a large editorial budget ensures that the *Mail* is a first class read and often sets the agenda for the day for the BBC and other TV stations' topical talk shows.

People often ask me about his retirement plans. 'They do not exist,' I tell them.

At this time I also took on a new role as chairman of the Parliamentary and Legal Committee of the Society of Editors. This body, which is run by the energetic and experienced Bob Satchwell as executive director, has a membership of more than 400 editorial executives from local, regional and national newspapers and from the main TV broadcasters – the BBC, ITV, ITN, and Sky. As such it is the only body that is able to speak for the whole industry. Therefore leading politicians, officials and policemen were all ready to attend our regular off-the-record lunches and tend to be less discreet than they are when they are reportable. I hope this is not another process which is ended as a result of the Leveson inquiry. So far the omens are good.

It was through the Society of Editors that I came to know Jack Straw, Labour's last Minister for Justice, quite well. As I have written earlier, his officials invited me to join the Libel Reform group which met on a regular basis at the Ministry. Since it included claimant lawyers, media lawyers, academics as well as senior editorial figures it never appeared to agree on anything – except the need for the reform of the laws to meet modern media needs.

Such a bill to reform the draconian and outdated laws of defamation has at last, after fourteen years of debate, made its way through Parliament. It promised some well overdue improvements but it took far too long to make its way through the mire that is modern politics. An unhelpful amendment tabled in the Lords by Lord Puttenham in an effort to force the government to bring in statutory control of the Press caused further and frustrating delay. Still, we got half-way there in the end.

The vexed question of Conditional Fee Arrangements, which allow successful claimant lawyers to charge the media firms that have allegedly libelled their clients, up to 100% increase on their fees, created a gravy train of incredible proportions for them and produced a chilling effect across the whole of the media. The costs of defending libel cases were way out of proportion to the damages awarded if the case was lost. We did eventually persuade Jack Straw that this was iniquitous and, towards the end of Labour's tenure he introduced a measure that, at a stroke, would have reduced the lawyers' uplift of their fees from 100% to 10%. This measure, vigorously opposed by nearly all the lawyers in and out of Parliament, was lost in the 'wash-up days' of the out-going Labour government and it took a further four years to reform it.

It was not all doom and gloom in the managing editor's office however and I had a delightful reminder of one of my best scoops when the British Library opened an exhibition of Front Pages to mark the centenary of the setting up of the national newspapers' industry body, the NPA. The Queen was invited to view the display which, of course, included my Man Is On The Moon front page. A little later at the event I was introduced to her and I found her remarkably well informed. She mentioned to me that the *Evening Standard* Front Page was actually printed in advance of Neil Armstrong's landing.

'But yours,' she said, 'recorded the real event as it happened.'

She asked me how many journalists were present at NASA headquarters in Houston on that day. More than three thousand.

'How on earth did you get the news back when there were no mobile phones then?' she asked.

We chatted about the way I had done it and I recalled to her that it took several days to get the news and pictures back of the conquest of Everest in her Coronation year. She nodded and said: 'Now it is a matter of seconds.'

She went on to ask how I got the colour pictures back to the UK as they could not, in those days, be wired and I was able to give her a brief account.

In my role as executive managing editor of the *Mail* I soon developed a 'pen pal' in Cherie Blair.

Mrs Blair, who was politically and naturally not a fan of the *Daily Mail*, used to complain every time we wrote about her. Sometimes she had a point, many other times she did not. It soon became obvious to me that, although allegedly a sharp lawyer, she had not mastered the fairly simple clauses of the Editors' Code of Practice, nor did she understand what was meant by a public place.

On one occasion she complained that we had run a picture of herself and her young son Leo at a football match and that this had invaded her privacy and that of her son. I had to point out that they were sitting in VIP seats at a high profile event where they could be seen by nearly 100,000 fans at the game as well as millions who watched on television when the cameras picked them out. You cannot have an expectation of privacy at such a public event. In all, between 2006 and 2010 Cherie complained to us and our sister papers, the *Mail on Sunday* and the *Evening Standard* about 40 times. Of mostly trivial complaints only seven ended in either an apology, a correction or legal damages.

While I think they were protective of their children's privacy the Blairs also were not above using the media to promote their family image when the right photo opportunity presented itself. I suspected that Cherie was driven more than anything else by her dislike of the *Mail* ethos and politics. She was never popular with the band of press photographers from whichever newspaper they worked for. They seemed to take a delight in photographing her looking bizarre or unkempt. There have been suggestions that this was deliberate. I could not comment on that but have you ever seen a published photograph of the former prime minister's wife looking glamorous?

I was often asked to negotiate with the BBC's press officers after the *Mail* had been strongly critical of something the BBC had done. Our conversations often revolved round the way the BBC had treated the *Mail*. But I always reminded them how much they gained from the *Mail Weekend* magazine, the country's most comprehensive and popular TV publication. I suppose those conversations helped take the tension away and two of the press officers I talked with have become firm friends – Sally Osman, now head of communications at Buckingham Palace, and Ed Williams, now with Edelman, the world's largest PR firm.

Meeting the Queen...

Robin Esser (left) with Kevin Beatty, CEO of DMG Media, and editor Paul Dacre. In the background is Peter Wright, former *Mail on Sunday* editor and now editor emeritus of the *Daily Mail*.

After looking at the 'Man Is On The Moon' front page, the Queen asked: 'How on earth did you get the news back when there were no mobile phones then?'

My job had its very entertaining moments. The *Mail* published an article by Iqbal Wahhab, then the editor and founder of *Tandoori* magazine. In it he was highly critical of the chicken marsala dishes so frequently provided by Indian restaurants all over Britain. As many of these were run by the Bangladeshi community they regarded it as an insult peddled by the *Mail*. Newsagents, many also run by Bangladeshi people throughout the land, boycotted the distribution of the *Daily Mail*.

I had to embark on a tour of the more sensitive mosques to explain that the view was not that of the *Mail* but of Iqbal who himself was of Bangladeshi origin, that he was an expert in his own field and that Indian restaurants everywhere could benefit from the publicity by improving their chicken marsala and telling their customers this is what they had done.

In one Glasgow mosque I was confronted by a group of young and fairly fanatical young men in white gowns. They were clearly not going to be mollified by my blandishments and wanted to push the idea of a total ban on the *Mail* throughout Glasgow. I was saved by an urbane and civilised senior academic from Glasgow University who arrived late and brought a much more reasonable voice to the debate.

I must have done a good job in the end as for several years after that I was asked to be a judge in the Curry Chef of the Year competition – at some cost to my digestive system.

Iqbal went on to found the Cinnamon Club in Westminster and then Roast restaurant in the Borough market. He was awarded the OBE for his efforts to help the Bangladeshi communities in Britain and he continues this valuable work to this day. He remains a firm friend and one of the most accomplished and charming people I have ever met.

Dealing with the Press Complaints Commission was high on my list of things to do. It seemed to me that the Editors Code of Practice was a very sensible attempt to raise the standards of all newspapers and magazines. The PCC was run by its chairman, the very able John Wakeham, now Lord Wakeham, former chief whip to Margaret Thatcher, ably helped by his director the very competent Mark Bolland.

When I began by dealing with the body the director was Guy Black – now Lord Black, a man of high integrity and a very good brain. While the first chairman, Lord Macgregor, had rather put his foot in it over the coverage of Princess Diana, not realising that she was an ace manipulator of the media in her own right, John Wakeham's tenure was sound and successful. He is a very canny operator and always thought long and hard about how what he said would go down with his audience. Admittedly he did not have the Human Rights Act, the Data Protection Act and other restrictive legislation to hamper him and he had attracted a panel of eminent people to sit upon the Commission, which had a lay majority but also a sensible representation of editors from national, regional and local papers and from magazines. None of these editors ever sat on complaints about their own publications or publications in the same group as their own.

Those who imagined the editors closed ranks over complaints about their rivals do not understand the nature of Fleet Street. Many of them would delight in finding against the editor of another paper. Alas John felt he had to do the honourable thing and resign when the scandal of the Enron payments to executives broke – he was on the Enron Board as a non-executive director and had to accept some responsibility for those rewards.

He was succeeded in the PCC job by Sir Christopher Meyer, a distinguished diplomat and our former ambassador in Washington. Christopher was an extremely able chairman of the PCC and his director was Tim Toulmin, who succeeded Guy Black in the role. There was one nervous time when Christopher published his controversial book about his time in Washington which contained several rather harsh judgments on how British politicians had failed to impress the Americans during their frequent visits to the States. The book, highly entertaining and amusing, caused most of the diplomatic establishment and Labour politicians to fall out with Christopher and it represented a problem for Fleet Street. Who could run extracts from a book written by the independent head of the self- regulation body which upheld Press standards?

The problem was solved when the *Daily Mail* and the Guardian shared the serialisation – a co-operation between two papers which are normally at daggers drawn and which was, I think, without precedent. In the book Christopher was particularly critical of the behaviour of John Prescott, the deputy prime minister. Prescott responded by categorizing Christopher as 'the Fop in red socks' a reference to Christopher's habit of invariably wearing such colourful footwear. In view of Prescott's shocking affair with his official diary secretary in tax payer's time in an office paid for by the tax payer and over a desk provided by the tax payer, I would choose the company of the red socked one over the red faced one any time.

A further testing moment came when the tragedy of Madeleine McCann, snatched away from her bed at the Algarve resort of Pria da Luz, hit the headlines.

Christopher's delightful wife, Catherine, who had suffered having her children taken off to Germany when she and her first husband divorced, had huge sympathy for the McCanns and was very supportive of them. When the McCanns found the coverage of the newspapers swinging towards the false theory of the Portuguese policeman in charge of the investigation that the McCanns themselves had a hand in their daughter's disappearance Christopher offered the PCC's services. However they chose to go down the libel route, being awarded considerable sums by the papers who had overdone the unsupportable Portuguese theory, which they gave to charities.

Now, after such a long time, that inquiry has been opened again by the British police in partnership with the Portuguese. However whatever is discovered, I think regrettably that a happy ending is almost impossible.

Christopher was succeeded by Lady Buscombe as head of the PCC. She had a very difficult time during which the PCC came under fire on a number of issues including, and quite unfairly, the phone hacking scandal. She was assured by the Met Police that they had thoroughly investigated the phone hacking at the *News of the Word* and she made this assurance public – only to be contradicted when it came out that there had been a cover-up. Lady Buscombe left the helm and was succeeded by Lord Hunt of the Wirral who showed a very steady hand indeed, despite the Leveson inquiry. But more of that anon.

Early on in my new role I was asked to serve on the D-Notice committee – proper name the Defence Press and Broadcasting Advisory Committee. This is a peculiarly British institution which is widely misunderstood. It does not slap 'D-notices' on publications but does advise media on matters that might compromise National Security if they were read by terrorists or other enemies. Editors are free to take that advice or ignore it, but as no editor would want to put anyone's life at risk, the advice is usually taken. The committee is comprised of officials from the Cabinet Office, the Home Office, the Ministry of Defence and the Foreign and

Commonwealth Office on the one side and representative of national newspapers, Scottish papers, local papers, book publishers and the BBC, ITN and Sky TV. Sitting between the two sides are the secretary and his deputy (when I was there it was Air Vice-Marshal Andy Vallance and Air Commodore David Adams) whose job it is to implement the committee's wishes.

As this is all voluntary and no one is forced to take advice this sat well within the boundaries of Press freedom and I felt the work was worthwhile as it certainly saved lives. I had many years attending the committee which met in my old stamping ground, the War Office, not much changed since my National Service days. When I eventually left the committee I think without precedent I was seen off with a glass or two and a wine decanter which had engraved on it 'SSHH! TOP SECRET! DPBAC1/11/12'.

During my time with the *Mail* I think I can claim to be one of the leading lights in the campaign to erect a monument to 'The Few', those fighter pilots, flying Hurricanes and Spitfires, who literally saved Britain from invasion by the Nazis in the Battle of Britain. Bill Bond, the inspirational man behind the Battle of Britain Historical Society which was set up to remind successive generations of that historic air battle in 1940, wrote to the *Daily Mail* asking for support for a fund to build a permanent memorial in London. The editor at once saw how this would appeal to *Daily Mail* readers and gave me the go-ahead to arrange for stories to be written and the campaign launched. The response from *Mail* readers was generous and quick and gave the Society the kick start it needed. Bill appointed Lord Tebbit as chairman of the fund and private donations carried the fund to the target figure of more than £1.5million. The Battle of Britain Monument was opened in London on the Embankment overlooking the River Thames and was unveiled on 18 September 2005, the 65th anniversary of the battle, by the Prince of Wales and the Duchess of Cornwall in the presence of many of the surviving 'Few'. The monument has a panelled granite structure 25 metres long which was originally designed as a smoke outlet for underground trains when they were powered by steam engines. A walkway was cut obliquely through the middle of the structure, and is lined with panels of high relief sculpture in bronze depicting scenes from the Battle of Britain. The centre piece is an approximately life sized sculpture of airmen scrambling for their aircraft during the battle. The outside of the monument is lined with bronze plaques listing all the airmen who took part in the battle on the allied side.

There was an unexpected sequel to this project when my wife and I hailed a black cab to attend the official opening. When I gave the driver our destination he told us that his wife's father had been one of the Battle of Britain pilots and he wondered if his name would be on the monument. I told him it certainly would and if he gave me his mobile number I would phone him to confirm after the ceremony.

'I'll take the wife to see it,' he said. 'She will be thrilled.' Of course his name was there and I duly confirmed it with the cab driver. By the way, he had waived the fare so we had a free ride to the monument.

During the exposure of the way some MPs had been feathering their nests in the incredibly lax rules that governed their expenses the *Mail* described the way in which Ed Balls and his wife, Yvette Cooper, had changed the designation of their two homes to enable them to claim huge sums on their expenses as 'milking the system'.

The inevitable letter of complaint came in with which I had to deal. I wrote back and in the course of the letter said, 'the public's view of the change of designation by Yvette Cooper of her 'second home' from Castleford to London, enabling both of you to claim £1,466 in mortgage interest was an act which most people might believe was "milking the system". In all this enabled you to claw back more than £300,000 from taxpayers. The description of your London home, shared with your three children from which they go to school as a second home is not how the everyday meaning of the phrase "second home" is generally interpreted.'

That ended the debate but at least the system of expenses has been tightened up so that some of the obvious loopholes are no longer there – but much more needs to be done. However it is not surprising that, after the exposure, many politicians would like to get their own back on the Press and see it under their ultimate control.

I have one correspondent who always sends me a copy of any letters she has sent to ministers, politicians, people in power. I do not get involved in her arguments – but I usually agree privately with everything she writes.

Among critical lefties the *Daily Mail*, which they rarely read, has a totally unjustified reputation for being, in Gregg Dyke's memorable phrase, 'hideously white'. Nothing could be further from the truth. The only criteria required of candidates for staff jobs is that they should be first class journalists.

In order to encourage as wide a possible pool from which the *Mail* can pick its reporters and sub editors I helped to develop the Journalism Diversity Fund, administered through the National Council for the Training of Journalists, the NCTJ. Set up in 2006 it has awarded bursaries to well over 100 young people from ethnic and poorer backgrounds to enable them to complete their training. Further efforts have been made by the *Mail* support of the *Asian Trader* group's Young Journalist of the Year contest which has thrown up some remarkable people from ethnic minorities – three winners of which have joined the staff of the *Mail* and are highly professional.

Journalism has always been an open profession in which you did not need an old school tie. The traditional way into the trade was via a local newspaper which you joined on leaving school and learnt your skills the hard way. Social and economic factors have changed all that and now the majority of entrants have some sort of college training.

Those from poorer families thus face financial stress and these two schemes help them. I am always encouraged by the number of young people who aspire to become newspaper journalists. The *Mail* runs an annual training scheme for 14 young reporters and sub-editors. More than a thousand applied for it in 2013.

Becoming a print journalist is still the accolade most aspiring journalists desire. After all anyone can write a blog, run an online commentary on anything. Only those trained to understand the disciplines of print and succeed in print can truly account themselves fully qualified. This is not a personal observation of someone who has been around a long time. I am indirectly quoting a 24 year old. I am often asked what makes someone a good candidate and I always say I ask them if they also are thinking of any other calling. If they say 'Well I thought I might become a vicar', I reply: 'Go and be a vicar then.' The determination to become a journalist is the first qualification any young person needs.

One day I was asked to entertain the Russian Oligarch Alexander Lebedev and his son Evgeny, who were introduced to the chairman of the *Mail* group and his wife through the *Tatler* editor Geordie Greig, now the successful editor of the *Mail on*

Sunday. The Lebedevs came into the office and I gave them a brief tour and answered their questions, many of which centred on the reasons for the success of the *Mail*. I must have impressed them more than I realised as they subsequently bought the *Evening Standard* and the two *Independent* newspapers and founded, *I*, the unusual potted edition of the main paper. I have always speculated there was an element of self- preservation in these purchases as I am sure even the thugs of Moscow would hesitate to assassinate the owner of influential newspapers in the West.

Lebedev is a courageous man who has used his great wealth to oppose the dictatorial regime of President Putin and to found a large number of excellent charities. With Russia's liberalising leader, Mikhail Gorbachev, he part owns the only significant critical paper in Russia, the *Novaya Gazeta*, which has seen several of its prominent reporters assassinated. However Putin appears determined to break Lebedev financially and an incident on Moscow TV where Lebedev came to blows with his debating opponent gave rise to a court case that threatened to put him in jail. In the end he was sentenced to community service.

However the pressure goes on to this day as the Kremlin continues to try to undermine and destroy his finances. Meanwhile his son Evgeny oversees the UK papers and, like his father, is a believer in a free Press. I suppose that you have to live under a controlled Press to recognise the benefit to the nation of a free one. That learning curve is something the British public has never experienced and I hope never will.

12

THE CHAINS TIGHTEN

The Leveson Inquiry was set up by David Cameron, a prime minister with many admirable qualities, but who, as I have written in the introduction, was rushed into the idea in the hope that it would cover up his lack of judgement in appointing Andy Coulson, former editor of the *News of the World* when it was indulging in phone hacking, as his communications chief and taking him to Number Ten when Cameron became prime minister.

The inquiry was based, as I have pointed out, on a lie: perhaps three lies, which Lord Justice Leveson appeared to swallow wholesale. The first lie was that the public had lost faith in the PCC self-regulation. There has never been any evidence of this, no polls, no dramatic loss in circulation, no reduction of readership of newspapers – in fact the opposite. Readership has increased.

The second lie was that phone hacking was widespread in the Press industry. Months of inquiry turned up little to support that contention. The third lie was that the *News of the World* had deleted messages on the murdered Millie Dowler's mobile phone giving her parents hope that she was still alive.

This story was carried on the *Guardian* front page. It was not until the police revealed that her phone automatically deleted messages that the lie was corrected by the *Guardian* – though not on the front page this time, as I have pointed out earlier.

In fact the Leveson Inquiry revealed much more about the dubious behaviour of our politicians and the Met Police than it did about the ethics of the Press as a whole.

The stupid idea of stretching the possible law-breaking of one tabloid Sunday newspaper into a witch hunt over the entire British Press was a massive miscalculation and dragged the fourth estate into a limbo from which it is struggling to free itself.

The Inquiry came back to bite Cameron, revealing his incautious closeness to the Rupert Murdoch empire and its chief executive in the UK, Rebekah Brooks .However a parade of pantomime celebrities appeared early before the good judge with whining complaints about the stories they would rather not have seen in the papers.

Some individuals have been badly treated by the Press. Of that there is no doubt. But to see the 'Hacked Off' movement, which wants statutory underpinning to regulation of the Press, being backed by that trio of upright citizens, Hugh Grant, Max Mosely and Steve Coogan, is surely one of the sickest jokes the British public has seen in a long time.

However the BBC, which is constitutionally critical of the Press and in particular the popular Press, wallowed in its coverage of the alleged malpractices.

The chilling effect the Leveson inquiry has had on freedom of speech is easy to see. But there were other, just as serious, consequences – unintentional though they may have been – to what was uncovered. The exposure of the pathetic way in which the political classes buttered up the Murdoch empire gave everyone a good laugh at the time. The neighbourly relationship between Rebekah Brooks and the Prime Minister will be remembered long after the present incumbent has left Number Ten. But the exposure of this cosiness and the exposure of the way in which the BskyB bid was handled has swept away much of what was left of the public's trust, after the expenses scandal, in politicians of all hues.

The Inquiry, helped by a national newspaper, exposed the lack of rigour with which the police pursued the illegal phone hacking at the *News of the World*. A failure of duty which, with no apparent logic, was blamed on the Press Complaints Commission which was never in a position to punish law-breaking. Top policemen resigned and some 175 officers pursued the cases that should have been pursued before but with a Stasi-like zeal which was out of proportion to the crimes committed. As the police, who regularly claim they are under-resourced, trawled though millions of News International e-mails how many trained officers were left to deal with the murderers, rapists, serious burglars and terrorists who roam our streets? Public safety was seriously put at risk.

I do not excuse the phone hackers for behaving as they did, but how deadly serious is the crime of listening to someone else's phone compared with murder, rape, burglary, assault and acts of terror-related killings?

A number of professional journalists were arrested at dawn in their houses, leaving their families traumatised and their wives in need of counselling. One journalist I know (and respect) watched helplessly as the police searched though his children's school satchels at six am. He had nothing to hide. He would have turned up at a police station at an appointed time. He certainly had no access to any material that the police did not already possess, which they must have known. He had been effectively 'chilled'.

'Chilling' is an appropriate word for the effect of the Inquiry on democracy and freedom of speech. And what has happened threatens the very existence of many local and regional newspapers which have never been involved in illegal behaviour but struggle to comprehend what draconian regulation is now threatened and struggle to imagine how they will afford to pay for such regulation.

As the former Lord Chief Justice has so rightly pointed out, this country deserves and expects a free Press. Much of the broadcast media is under government supervision. The Press, both in print and online, is so far free from political over-view and must remain so.

Didn't Lord Leveson read the Lord Chief Justice's speech on the freedom our community expects?

Editors are confused about what is considered to be in the public interest. Judges vary tremendously about what is and what is not in the public interest. One interpretation of a fairly recent case seemed to suggest that if you are the captain of an international football team your off-field behaviour is in the public interest but if you are merely a member of the squad it is not.

The task of defending Press freedom has grown more and more complicated – and interesting – as the politicians have increasingly put pressure on the media to conform to their ideas of regulation (or control) and statute after statue has passed through parliament limiting the ability of journalists to do the job for which they are trained – which is routing out scandal and the abuse of tax payers' funds and generally keeping the public informed of what is going on in their name. And also, of course, entertaining readers with gossip, fashion, trends and the lighter side of life.

There are those who believe that the exposure of the expenses scandal involving members of parliament has given an added spur to these attempts to curb the media. The idea that the general public had 'lost trust' in self-regulation was invented by the Prime Minister. There was no evidence that this was so. No surveys, no vox pops, no visible signs that the public had stopped reading newspapers in printed form, on tablets and on line.

At the time of the Inquiry the former Press Complaints Commission chairman, Sir Christopher Meyer, wrote in a piece about Prince Harry's naked larking with a bunch of girls in his Las Vegas suite for the *Huffington Post* in 2012:

Unlike phone hacking, a criminal offence for investigation by the police, the Prince Harry *affaire* is stuffed with pertinent issues for Lord Justice Leveson as he ponders the future of Press regulation. Two things should strike him forcefully. Firstly, Press regulation is becoming more complex by the day as the dislocation grows between the unregulated internet and the regulated media. Secondly, the Press Complaints Commission (PCC) is back in fashion. Why? Because it is needed. As of writing, it has received almost a thousand complaints about the naked Harry photos published in the *Sun*. In the ensuing debate, commentators have invoked the clauses of the Editors' Code of Practice dealing with privacy, as well as the PCC's rulings over twenty years, an invaluable archive. How foolish it was to launch the Inquiry on the careless assumption that the PCC was not fit for purpose; and that Judge Leveson had no need for an independent member of the Commission, past or present, on his panel of assessors.

The media in this country is not free – as it is in the USA. Television companies and radio are regulated and supervised by a government body – OfCom. The BBC is constantly under the lash as it is funded by the tax payer via the government and newspapers are regulated, not only by restrictive laws but by a system of self-regulation which the politicians keep trying to ratchet up. Add to this several restricting acts of parliament like the Data Protection Act, the Harassment Act and the Bribery Act, not to mention the Human Rights Act and you can see the creeping claws of State control. If this trend continues the public's right to know what goes on in their name, and with their money will be eroded on a local, regional and national level. The word democracy will have a hollow ring.

Kangaroo courts are springing up all around us. Parliamentary select committees on media matters abound and the Leveson Inquiry was the last straw. What is now clear is that those running the Inquiry had only the sketchiest idea of how the Press works and the scale on which it operates. The *Mail*, for example, prints more than a million items of news in a year and MailOnLine and Mail Plus even more. In that context the stories that are controversial and are seriously complained about are few and far between. Judge Leveson wanted to visit the *Daily Mail* before he sat in the Inquiry – as I believe he visited other newspapers. I was put in charge of the visit. The first suggestion from his office was he would come at ten in the morning.

'Well I will be here, but not many others will be,' I said, explaining to his staff that daily papers are made at night. I suggested 8pm would be a more rewarding time for him to see how a newspaper was put together. In the end he came at 6pm and stayed until about 8pm by which time four pages of an 80-page paper had been completed.

He was surprised to hear that the editor would still be around at 10pm to check the first edition and make changes and improvements.

His panel of 'assessors' who sat with him during the inquiry did not have a single journalist from the popular papers on it nor, as Sir Christopher pointed out above, a single member of the PCC. What it did have was the presence and influence of Sir David Bell, one of the leading lights of the Media Standards Trust, which appears to back state interference with regulation.

In 2011 I was elected as president of the Society of Editors. It proved to be a challenging year. To emphasize the Society's dedication to Press freedom I persuaded the board to hold our November annual conference at the site where Magna Carta was signed. We checked in to the Runnymede Hotel and invited a number of high profile figures to come and speak, including Ken Clarke, the Justice Minister, Dominic Grieve, the Attorney General, Lord Patten, the chairman of the BBC Trust, Lord Hunt, the man charged with designing a successor to the PCC and Lord Justice Leveson. The Inquiry judge was the only one to decline, which I thought was an opportunity missed since we have so many editors and senior editorial executives among our members.

Patten, Clarke and Grieve all said they were opposed to legislation to control the Press which was good news, as was Michael Gove's later sterling defence and William Hague's announcement that he opposed any statutory control. In fact, of course, newspapers are controlled by the law, as I have mentioned before, and they can be fined huge sums for breaches of the law. What we do not need is any extensions of that iron grip.

Ken Clarke arrived at Runnymede a little before he was due to speak and sat outside the conference room where I joined him. The Information Commissioner, Chris Graham, who, along with his predecessor, had been campaigning for prison sentences to be available for breaches of the Data Protection Act – something the media was very nervous about as almost any inquiry by a journalist risks being classified as a breach of the DPA – came up to us and made his pitch for prison punishment, pointing out that magistrates courts only fined offenders a small sum when found guilty.

'If you think I am going to stuff my jails full of people who break your act you have another think coming,' Ken Clarke roared.

'There is no room to lock up the murderers, rapists and terrorists.'

'Well the courts fine them derisory sums,' protested Graham.

'We've cured that,' said Ken Clarke. 'We have removed the ceiling magistrates courts can levy on fines. They can impose up to £100,000 now!'

To be fair the Information Commissioner has always said he is not after journalists and I believe him. What I do not know is that the next commissioner, or the one after that, will have the same view.

Then, a journalist seeking an ex-directory telephone number to put an allegation to someone will risk prosecution and possibly a jail sentence if that early inquiry ultimately proves not to be 'in the public interest'. But how on earth can he or she know if the tip being followed will end up as a story in the public interest before the answers have been given?

Michael Gove was right – and brave – in 2012 insofar as he spotlighted the chilling effect the Leveson Inquiry had on freedom of speech. But there were other, just as serious, consequences to what was uncovered. The exposure of the pathetic way in which the political classes buttered up Rupert Murdoch gave everyone a very good laugh at the time. But the exposure of this cosiness and the exposure of the way in which the BSkyB bid for more control by Murdoch was handled, swept away much of what was left of the public's trust in politicians of all complexions. This was patently bad for democracy.

Unless the people can trust that those elected to run the country in their name will behave responsibly the rise of those who support the far right or the far left, which we have seen throughout Europe, will happen here. Unless a majority of the population turns out to vote in a general election what *representation* will they have in Parliament? The Inquiry, as I have said, helped by a national newspaper, exposed the lack of rigour with which the police pursued the illegal phone hacking at the *News of the World*. A failure of duty for which no senior policeman has publically shouldered the blame. As the police, who regularly claim they are under-resourced, trawled though millions of News International e-mails how many trained officers were left to deal with more serious crimes?

Then we had the ludicrous and destructive report from Elizabeth Filkin, the former Parliamentary Standards Commissioner, on the new rules about police talking to the Press, a report sparked by the atmosphere the Inquiry generated. If followed to the letter these rules interfere with the free flow of information on a local level which allow the local Press to inform their readers of what is happening in their name and in the public interest in their community. Now people can be arrested in secret and removed from their homes without any of their neighbours knowing. Is that the sort of country in which we want to live? Chilling is an appropriate word for the effect on democracy and freedom of speech

As I have written, the former Lord Chief Justice, Judge Igor Judge, so rightly pointed out, this country deserves and expects a free Press. Though the broadcast media is under government supervision through OfCom, the body Leveson apparently thought might help to regulate the Press, it failed to prevent the undeserved traducing of Lord McAlpine's reputation by the infamous Newsnight programme, which caused him to be named on the internet as a paedophile when he was obviously totally innocent.

The Press, both in print and online, is so far free from political over-view and it must remain so. The British people have never lived under a totalitarian regime so they have no experience of a fettered Press. They are not vocal in supporting it. But it is time they awoke to the on-going efforts of some politicians to curb and control the media to ensure they get an easier ride.

Yes, some individuals have been unfairly monstered by over-the-top tactics by a few journalists. Although we should all feel sorry for them and ashamed of the rogues who perpetrated those sins, and make every effort to temper such unacceptable inquiries, I firmly believe that the free Press benefits millions of ordinary people and therefore it is a freedom that must be preserved, warts and all.

A great deal of fuss is also made of the mindless pursuit of celebrities by the paparazzi. But how would a law curb them? Many of them are foreign nationals and even if the British papers decline to buy their pictures they would not go away as their main markets are abroad in European and American magazines.

Journalism is global in more ways than one.

The lawyers – from articled clerks to eminent judges – rule this country and they have developed the compensation culture to feather their own nests. The panoply of QCs and solicitors, all paid for by the poor old tax payers, that the Leveson Inquiry attracted might well have been highly qualified in the law, but what did they know about journalism? Let the Press do what it is supposed to do – telling people what they ought and need to be told. All freedoms have their downside. The upsides are more important to a democratic society.

The Leveson report demonstrates how the eminent judge continued to fail to understand what a free Press means and to overestimate the scale of any alleged wrong-doing by a minority of journalists. After all there are bad apples in any barrel. The Hacked Off brigade are themselves a vocal but small number of people who made a big noise.

One of its most outspoken leaders has been the actor, Hugh Grant. It is no wonder he would like to control the Press that carried the story of his being arrested for consorting with a prostitute in Los Angeles.

Another enthusiast for repression is Max Mosley, whose sordid and sadistic meetings with ladies of the night were also exposed by the newspapers. Would you not have thought that these pillars of rectitude would have been shamed into silence? What about the millions of people who have benefitted from campaigns and investigative journalism into the wrong-doings of those in public employment? What about the elderly who have been let down in so called 'care' homes? What about the scandalous situation in some NHS hospitals that have let their patients die through lack of care – sometimes through simply not giving them enough water to drink? What about the tax payer who has to stump up for criminals who are in jail but continue to claim benefits? What about the public who have discovered that some MPs ripped them off over their expenses? What about the dreadful behaviour of the head of the Co-Op bank arrested for allegedly buying drugs with the bank's money and fiddling his expenses? Would the widespread abuse of young girls in Rochdale have come to light without a free and unfettered Press? The list goes on and on.

Leveson, as I observed before, said the police investigated the phone hacking first time round at the *News of the World* with integrity as they were concentrating on anti-terrorism activity. That was breath taking. He did not explain why, if that was the case, three top men from the Met resigned. Nor why, when their neglect of their duty to enforce the law was revealed, they put more than a hundred detectives on the case. What happened to the anti-terrorism activity then?

Another question Leveson totally ignored is the uncontrolled nature of the internet. He ignored it because he knows his solutions will not work on it. His report refers only to England and Wales – not even to Scotland, or the Channel Islands. The press industry – which is expected to pay for the 'independent' regulator – has been poorly treated by this sham. I hope it will survive the challenge. However it is not all over yet. The prospect of statutory intervention will raise its head again. The Labour party would love to control what they have always regarded as 'the Tory Press'. We have Alastair Campbell's word on that.

For once we can believe him.

Meanwhile the whole Inquiry, which was started as a political ploy, lapsed back into politics with its uninformed, tortuous and now largely discredited recommendations. Wisely the newspaper industry recruited a canny politician and lawyer, Lord Hunt of the Wirral, to come up with an improved system of self-regulation, backed by independent people of upright standing.

David Hunt's suggestions mapped a sensible path for the future and perhaps the Press can get on with more serious matters like defending little people against the over mighty state. The dangers represented by the Leveson recommendations were amply demonstrated when the Culture Secretary's spin doctor and the Number Ten chief of communications, Craig Oliver, both threated the *Daily Telegraph* with implementation of statutory control when that newspaper probed the complications of former culture secretary Maria Miller's expenses claims. Claims which ultimately caused her resignation. A foretaste of the control the politicians would love to exercise over a free Press.

I do not entirely blame Lord Justice Leveson for the trouble he has visited on the Press and the public. After all he is a judge and judges deal with law. Only natural that his mind would work that way. The blame must surely lie with those who set up the Inquiry without thinking where it would lead.

We ended up with an over-the-top police force, arresting more journalists than Robert Mugabe has in Zimbabwe, torturing those with extended bail and re-questioning month after month, arresting senior officers who have given their lives to serving the force and are now in fear of speaking to the media at all.

We have heard some civilised people actually calling for statutory control of the Press and even the so called Liberal party, which should believe in free expression and liberty, at one time backing that call. And we have ended up with regulation (albeit self-regulation) that puts the media in Britain at a commercial and editorial disadvantage over the internet and the newspaper online sites which stem from America where there is no regulation.

Incredibly a group of politicians met in the Opposition Leader's office over a midnight pizza with members of the Hacked Off group present but no one from the media industry and came up with a plan that is unacceptable to the Press, probably illegal under both EU and English law, and which is scorned by international opinion. However they drew up a Royal Charter that would put the Press under threat of ultimate political control. The vast majority of newspapers, local, regional and national, and magazines of all types in Great Britain have refused to recognise or sign up to this 'Charter'.

And then, through a limited exposure by the Serious Organised Crime Agency but urged on by a parliamentary committee, it emerged that phone hacking on a much wider scale has long been practiced by legal firms, insurance companies and other blue-chip companies – and even perhaps by firms employed by the government.

As much as 80% of phone hacking has been by these companies or by private investigators acting for them.

Leveson, it transpired, was told about this but chose to ignore it, in a very judge-like way, by saying it was not part of his remit. But it has absolutely destroyed the point of his Inquiry and its point as it appears to show there is one law for the Press and another for those who were hacking elsewhere.

How many of those hackers were arrested, put on bail for three years? Tried in a court of law? In fact only one amusing thing emerged from Lord Leveson's Inquiry- the idea that you can take a girl you fancy off to a romantic Greek island to 'discuss' whether you should have an affair with her or not... which was the excuse put forward by a leading counsel for the complainants and a leading lawyer for the Inquiry who got together rather too cosily towards the end of the process.

Can the Press in Britain survive the unequal struggle that has been thrust upon it by the failure of the Met Police to arrest and pursue a number of possible law-breakers at News International? It is not all over yet. Hacked Off have lost some of their credibility and the increasing exaggeration of the language they are using shows they have realised their case for shackling the Press is not so easily won.

The politicians keep shifting their point of view in vain attempts to capture the public's attention and re-capture their trust. Alas they have forced the Queen to sign that Royal Charter that would allow politicians to have a say in what the papers print, essentially a set-up approved by politicians and Hacked Off with no regard to the views of the media industry. Instead the Press has reformed its self - regulatory body, under an independent judge, Sir Alan Moses, so that it has far greater powers than the PCC and can fine publishers up to a million pounds for serious failings to keep to the Editors Code of Practice.

Even this, in my opinion, is a step too far but I believe it is better than State control. Even the former culture minister, Maria Miller, said that the government should let the Press get on with its own self-regulation. Alas not long later the Prime Minister returned to the subject suggesting the Press should sign up to the Royal Charter before an even worse proposal is invented. Thus self-contradictory was our government even though Mr Cameron and Ms Miller belong to the same political party. Further the Royal Charter, which is still extant, creates one law for journalists and another law for everyone else. What other organisation or individual has to face exemplary damages in the libel court and is liable to pay the costs of the other side, even if they win their case?

This is not just my opinion. This is what Bob Satchwell, the executive director of the Society of Editors, a body that represents all the media, thinks:

'In essence the Royal Charter is part of a 40 year campaign by politicians to restrict the Press. There has been no statutory involvement by the state in Press regulation since 1695 when the Licensing Act was abolished. This reflects the special role of a free Press in the functioning of a democracy.

'The Press is there to scrutinise those in positions of power. It could not fulfil that role if those it was scrutinising had authority, however apparently limited, over it. The impact on a free society would be incalculable. The overwhelming majority of the Press disagree with government about the *principle* of statutory underpinning to allow any element of the state a role in the regulation of the Press.

'The Royal Charter would give politicians control over Press regulation in the future for precisely the reason that its proponents claim that it protects Press freedom. If regulation cannot be changed without a two thirds majority of both Houses of Parliament it also means that two thirds of parliament could vote to bring in much stronger control of regulation and even begin to control content.

'What Leveson and supporters of the Royal Charter fail to address is that all but one of the other inquiries into Press behaviour since the Second World War stopped short of statutory involvement because they realised that they must not restrict the freedom of the Press.

'In addition, the charter is fraught by controversy about the process by which it was created, which is subject to judicial review, and the process of setting up a recognition body is clearly fraught with practical difficulties. These issues may also be subject to legal challenge. This contrasts sharply with the sensible and steady progress that is being made towards the creation of the Independent Press Standards Organisation – IPSO – by the newspaper and magazine industry. Leveson said the best outcome of his inquiry would be the establishment of a self-regulatory system by the Press. That is precisely what IPSO is.

'Leveson also said it needed to have the confidence of politicians and the public.

'As IPSO is supported by more than 90 per cent of the newspaper and magazine industry, the industry by implication rejects the Royal Charter system. In a survey, a clear majority of the public said they did not want politicians to have any say in Press regulation. That means IPSO is nearer to Leveson's recommendations than the Royal Charter and the underlying proposal for regulation. Only politicians and pressure groups which do not like a vociferous popular Press want the charter.

'As politicians are riding roughshod over the views of the *whole* of the Press you will forgive us for thinking that it is surely a sign of what they are trying to achieve. Bear in mind that the Leveson inquiry was set up hurriedly in response to a politically motivated campaign to restrict Rupert Murdoch's ownership of BSkyB. The Prime Minister was acutely embarrassed by the phone hacking revelations – the worst of which, Millie Dowler, later proved to be not quite as reported – and also by his employment of a former editor of the *News of the World* as his Press secretary.

'The fact is that the Press has been subjected to judicial and police inquiries on an *unprecedented* scale. If that can be prompted by political *embarrassment* it is not difficult to see what politicians might do if they had control of Press regulation. Topping that, the Royal Charter proposals would allow courts to impose exemplary damages on newspapers which lose libel cases – and to make them pay all the costs even if they win! That is nothing more than shotgun legislation tacked on to the Crime and Courts Act 2013 in the midst of a party political row. Initially proposed as a carrot to tempt the industry in, it is almost certainly contrary to European law.

'Used as a punishment for refusal to sign up to a regulator approved by Parliament, these proposals to levy heavy fines and one-way costs orders fundamentally go against the long-established principles that the loser-pays and justice being fair to all.

'It remains that the Royal Charter arbitration system does not meet the concerns of regional and local publishers. Under the scheme, publishers would have to bear their own costs, the costs of the arbitration itself and the costs and expenses of the complainant could be awarded against them.

'Press freedom is not ours to give away and the case of a journalist being detained at Heathrow airport under anti-terrorism laws indicates the obvious lesson – that powers granted to the government for one reason often get abused for the purposes of others. The Press continues to play a vital role in bringing to account human rights abuses and the protection of national security secrets should never be used as an excuse to intimidate the Press into silence.

Whatever the rights or wrongs of publication of information about intelligence gathering, the government should remember that *journalism is not terrorism*.

'Free speech is vital for any free and democratic country. It sends a dangerous precedent to the rest of the world if the UK Government continues to press for involvement in the regulation of the Press. Press freedom is not merely the reserve of the Press that we like. Nor is it reserved solely for the journalists who hold officials to account and uncover that which others would prefer them not to know. A vibrant, vociferous and free and *popula*r Press, read by millions, is part of our way of life.

'And this dispute is not just about national newspapers. A free Press is just as important to people outside London, in cities, towns and rural villages, as it is for those who walk the streets and corridors of power. That is why newspapers and magazines are united in their rejection of a Royal Charter that undermines Press freedom and are generally as one in their support for the establishment of the new Independent Press Standards Organisation.'

Trenchant but true.

Unfortunately the Royal Charter gives a sombre message to the Commonwealth. I am a trustee of the Commonwealth Press Union which has fought for

Press freedom in those countries for years. So I realise only too well – though our narrow minded politicians did not – that our Queen is also the Queen of the Commonwealth and some of the more despotic heads of those countries rubbed their hands in glee that Her Majesty – under duress from a few Privy Councillors who are politicians – has signed away Press freedom and is 'on their side' at supressing any criticism or exposure of their corruption.

The police use of the Regulation of Investigatory Powers Act (RIPA) to harry and probe into journalistic sources has been yet another worrying intrusion into Press freedom. As Lord Rothermere said at the 2014 Press Ball in aid of the journalists charity 'never have journalists been so underrated and under attack'.

According to *Press Gazette*, the industry's trade journal, more than 25 police forces have refused to provide details of their use of RIPA under the Freedom of Information Act, some saying it would cost too much to find the information. Others have used the excuse of protecting 'national security' or the need to protect their tactics from criminals.

There appears to be no evidence of attention by the police to the sanctity of journalists' sources, nor for the role of whistle-blowers who are also supposed to be protected by the law.

Parliament clearly intended the Act as a weapon to be used against terrorism. But journalists are not terrorists.

In the two matters that have made headlines, the so-called 'Plebgate' affair and the Huhne speeding points case, journalists were targeted without any apparent suggestion of criminality on their part or that national security was involved. Every police force in the UK is being asked by a parliamentary committee to reveal how many times they have secretly snooped on journalists by obtaining their telephone and email records without their consent.

Keith Vaz, chairman of the Home Affairs Select Committee, said he wanted a detailed breakdown of police use of the Regulation of Investigatory Powers Act to force telecoms companies to hand over phone records without customers' knowledge. His intervention came after it emerged that police investigating the former MP Chris Huhne's speeding fraud secretly obtained a *Mail on Sunday* reporter's phone records without his consent despite laws protecting journalistic confidential sources. The newspaper said it had learnt that officers from Kent police used powers designed for anti-terrorism to identify a source they had failed to secure through a court application. In a strong leading article, it said the revelation demonstrated that the law was giving 'officials frightening and near-totalitarian powers'. It said police were using these secret powers to 'wrongfully' seize the phone records of thousands of innocent people.

It was the second time in one month that revelations emerged of the police secretly ordering phone companies to hand over journalists' phone bills and details of their calls, fuelling fears that media organisations will not be able to protect sources, particularly police whistle-blowers.

In late 2014 it emerged accidentally that the Metropolitan police had obtained the *Sun* news desk telephone records and those of its political editor, Tom Newton Dunn, to try to identify who had leaked the Plebgate story about the former Tory chief whip Andrew Mitchell's altercation with police at the gates of Downing Street. Kent police used RIPA laws after the Crown Prosecution Service applied for disclosure of material from the *Mail on Sunday* in an effort to identify the source who was the basis of stories about the Huhne affair.

The Crown Prosecution Service also wanted disclosure of material they believed had been provided by Constance Briscoe, a barrister and part-time judge who was jailed for trying to pervert the course of justice as part of the investigation into Huhne. The application was made under the Police and Criminal Evidence Act (Pace), which enshrines the principle of journalistic privilege and allows journalists and their employers to make representations to the court to protect their sources. On this occasion the judge ruled that the *Mail on Sunday* did have to disclose material but with names of sources edited out. Some of Briscoe's emails in relation to the speeding fraud referred to her having a police source, and Mr Justice Sweeney subsequently ordered that a police force should investigate whether she had compromised the investigation into Huhne's speeding ticket.

Unknown to the *Mail on Sunday*, Kent police secretly went to their journalist's mobile phone provider and ordered the release of records. They did not use Pace, which requires the police to go to court, but RIPA to get the records. RIPA could be used with approval from an officer of superintendent level or above, and did not require the police to disclose their intentions to snoop on journalists.

'They trawled through thousands of confidential records called by journalists from a landline at the busy news desk going back an entire year, covering hundreds of stories unrelated to the Huhne case,' the *Mail on Sunday* claimed. The paper said the source of its story was identified by police to be a freelance journalist in Cornwall, Andrew Alderson, a first class reporter who used to work for the *Sunday Express* when I was its editor, and details of telephone calls and emails between him and the *Sun* news editor David Dillon were passed to Huhne's defence lawyers. Police files included an entry which read: 'Landline attributed to David Dillon for the period 14/11/2011 to 13/11/2012. Checked for contact with all numbers'.

Keith Vaz said RIPA was not fit for purpose and needed 'total refurbishment'. He said: 'It is important that the public and parliamentarians get statistics on the number of times it is being used and how it is being used without journalists having to submit freedom of information requests. All kinds of mistakes are being made. Anecdotally we've heard of local authorities using it to check people's addresses when parents make applications for schools.

'I am writing to them, each of the police forces, to ask how many times they've used RIPA powers and where. I'd like it broken down by profession.'

He said the use of it against journalists struck 'a serious blow against Press freedom'. Vaz said he was suggesting to the select committee that they call on the Interception of Communication Commissioner to answer questions on the use of RIPA and its justification. Kent police believe the use of RIPA rather than Pace, which protects journalists, was justifiable. A spokesman told the *Mail on Sunday*: 'These applications were proportionate, lawful, necessary and were relevant lines of inquiry for the investigation and the facts were made available to the court and defence.'

Gavin Millar QC, who acted for *Mail on Sunday* publisher Associated Newspapers, and who is supporting an application to the European court of human rights to investigate British laws that allow GCHQ and police to secretly snoop on journalists, said he was alarmed by the police interventions in both the Huhne and Plebgate cases.

'This is a speeding points case. Plebgate is a case about a low-level officer leaking some information not for payment but with whistle-blower intentions.

The crimes being investigated in both these cases are not serious, they are not terrorism and they are not organised crime. There is no justification for using RIPA. It gives an insight into how freely they use this, but how can we have a debate about it unless they are transparent about it?'

He said journalists now kept so much source material electronically that it was a 'win-win' for police to use RIPA to get access.

'They are getting the information without having to do the work and in secret, taking a shortcut without having to go before a judge and justify it and give journalists an opportunity to defend the confidentiality of their sources,' said Millar.

Until and unless RIPA is revised freedom of the Press, which is the freedom of expression, will be severely curtailed in this country.

All this pressure finally had a positive result early in 2015 when the Interception of Communications Commissioner, Sir Anthony May, said the Home Office guidelines on the use of RIPA did not provide 'adequate safeguards' to protect journalists' sources. He said police should not intercept journalists' phone records unless a judge had given them the green light. The Prime Minster, David Cameron, then agreed to introduce such safeguards to prevent the police from abusing anti-terrorist legislation to pry on the Press. Another step in the right direction.

The Press of course itself is not always at one in its opinions and attitudes. The *Guardian* and occasionally the *Independent* often argue with the rest of the newspapers and publishers on a sensible way forward. The *Guardian*, which hates the popular and the more successful newspapers, rarely coincides with the rest of the industry in deciding which direction regulation should go. But there is something healthy about an industry that cannot agree among itself. And recent events – such as when the *Guardian* was forced by the Prime Minister to destroy some of their Wikileaks material provided by the renegade Edward Snowdon – have dramatically shown what politicians would like to do to newspapers.

It was sad that it took the murderous attack by Al Qaeda on the satirical magazine *Charlie Hebdo* in Paris for the Prime Minster and the Chancellor of Germany to issue a statement that finally confirmed their belief that freedom of expression must be maintained.

David Cameron said: 'We should never give up the values we believe in and defend as part of our democracy and civilisation – believing in a free Press, in freedom of expression, is the right of people to say and write what they believe.'

A pity he did not say this before setting up the Leveson Inquiry.

The final farce in this litany of incompetence came with the 'hacking trial' — a trial that dragged on and on, again at huge expense to the tax payer. Thank goodness for a sensible jury that threw out the majority of charges, only finding the former editor of the *News of the World* and David Cameron's communications chief at Number Ten guilty of phone hacking.

If democracy is to survive in this country and politicians are to be held accountable to the taxpayer, the Press, all of it, must remain free. What is needed is what has been promised by Sajid Javid, the Minister for Culture Media and Sport – a Bill of Rights entrenching freedom of expression for ever and echoing America's First Amendment.

It is in everybody's interests – even those members of Hacked Off if only they could think about it calmly and logically. But meanwhile the Crusaders are all still in chains even if we end up with self- fastening ones.

I still love journalism and newspapers at their best. I suppose I will never retire completely – like an old soldier I will just fade away. But it has been a great ride and my fervent hope is that newspapers, in all their forms, local, regional, and national, serious and unabashedly popular, will continue to entertain but above all be a thorn in the sides of cheats, wrong doers, those who abuse the young and the old, and the hypocrisy of those in power.

#

Lightning Source UK Ltd.
Milton Keynes UK
UKOW05f0504190516

274557UK00015B/296/P